A REAL G GUIDE

to Agile Project Documents

Agile Project Management, Technical Writing, the Document Life Cycle, and How a Real Gorilla Deals with This Marriage Made in Hell

Mark Williams

Printed by Create Space

Copyright©2015 Mark Williams

All rights reserved. No part of this book, or any part of the 12 worksheets that come with this book (available through e-mail which is given in the "Building Documents-The Gorilla Way" section) may be reproduced or transmitted in any form, or by any means, electronic, mechanical photocopying, recording, copy and pasting, or otherwise, without written consent of the author-that's me.

The information in this book, including the 12 worksheets available by e-mail, are provided "as is" without warranty of any kind, either expressed or implied, including without limitation any warranty concerning the accuracy, completion, and adequacy of any and all of the information contained in the book and worksheets, or the results to be obtained from using this information and material. Neither the author nor the printer will be responsible for any claims attributable to errors, omissions, or other inaccuracies in the information contained in the book or the 12 worksheets that come with it. In no event will the author or printer be liable for direct, indirect, special, incidental, or consequential damages arising out of the use of the information contained in this book or the 12 worksheets.

The Excel Spreadsheet:

The excel spreadsheet with the 12 tabs (worksheets) are the heart and soul of this book. They represent what I use on current projects. However, they were built over the course of eight years prior to my current job, as was this book, and reflect an average of best practices and processes I know that work now and have worked. With each project, they are modified and optimized to produce the best possible results. To understand them, you must have some knowledge of workflows, both electronic and paper, and the Agile SDLC and document life cycle.

As mentioned in the "All Rights Reserved" statement, you can e-mail me directly to get your spreadsheets by using the email in the "Building Documents-The Gorilla Way" section. Follow the directions. I use a commercial e-mail and do not sell, pass on, or spam these emails. Once the spreadsheet is sent, we delete the email. You should have your file within a few hours.

Thank you,

Mark

DISCLAIMER	7
WHAT IS A GORILLA?	7
PURPOSE	8
What This Book Does	9
What This Book is Not	10
A Writing Book	*10*
Long	*10*
An Agile Documentation Book	*11*
A Help-You-Do-Everything Book	*12*
COMPARATIVE DOCUMENTATION PROJECTS	12
Aerospace Company Tech Pub Projects	13
Agile Projects	13
WHY USE PROFESSIONAL TECHNICAL WRITERS?	14
Top Eight Reasons (Not All-Inclusive)	14
MINIMALISM SAVES MONEY	16
Tactical Minimalism	17
Strategic Minimalism	17
Culprits	18
Replacing Text with Graphics	20
Considerations	*21*
A Case Study . . . of a Sort	21
ORDER OF CONCERNS PARADIGM	23
The Four Higher-Order Concerns	24
The Four Lower-Order Concerns	24
TECHNICAL EDITORS	25
Responsibilities	25
Background	26
EDITING METRICS	26
Why One Dedicated Editor is Optimal	27
TECHNICAL WRITERS	30
Background	31
Duties	32
What They Are Not	32
A Word on Faux Tech Writers	33

TECHNICAL EDITS: THE SUBJECT MATTER EXPERT (SME) 35
- TECHNICAL WRITER AS SME 36

SPREADSHEETS EMAIL 36

BUILD DOCUMENTS-THE GORILLA WAY 37
- DETERMINE THE DOC PACK 37
- ASSIGN AUTHORS 39
- ASSIGN AUTHORIAL TEAMS AND OTHER ROLES 40
- AUTHORIAL TEAM SIZE 40
- COMPLETE THE DOC PREP CHECKLIST 42

THE GORILLA BUILD/REVIEW PROCESS 43
- THE DOC PREP CHECKLIST 45
- THE BUILD/REVIEW CYCLE (BRC) 49
- DATA-SLIM THE DOC PACK 53
  - *Gorillas' Data-Slim Steps 54*
  - *Data-Slim Exceptions 55*
  - *Gorilla Hopes for Data-Slim 55*

ONCE DEVELOPMENT STARTS 56
- GORILLAS DO NOT WAIT 58
- REVIEW CYCLES 60
- MEETINGS 61
- UPDATES 61
- UPDATE MANAGEMENT 62
- THE ONLINE DOCUMENT PACKAGE 64
  - *Combine All the Word Documents—If Possible 64*
  - *Example of an Online Doc Package 65*
  - *Combine the User Guide and Training Materials 65*
- GORILLA RULES FOR PHASING DOCUMENTS 68

PHASED DOCUMENTATION 72
- MAINTAINING DOCUMENTS AFTER DEPLOYMENT OR FINAL DELIVERY 73

SPECIAL CONSIDERATIONS FOR THE USER GUIDE 75
- WILL THE HELP BE EMBEDDED WITH THE APPLICATION OR IN ONE PLACE? 75
  - *One-Place Pros 75*
  - *One-Place Cons 76*
  - *Embedded-Help Pros 76*
  - *Embedded-Help Cons 77*
- CONTEXT-SENSITIVE HELP (CSH) 77

PLANNING AND ESTIMATING TOOLS: USER STORIES TO MAN-HOURS 79

USER GUIDE	80
INSTALLATION GUIDE	81
FACTORS THAT DETERMINE CREATE-BUILD-COMPLETE (CBC) TIMES	82
TEST RUNS FOR CBC TIMES	83

DOCUMENT QUALITY LEVEL 83

CHARACTERISTICS OF A C+ DOCUMENT	85

WRITING: CONVENTIONS, PHILOSOPHY, AND STYLE 86

PHILOSOPHIES	86
Client-Centred Writing: Audience Analyses	*86*
Tactical Minimalism	*87*
TECHNIQUES	92
SENTENCES	94
GORILLA PICKS ON WRITING STYLE	96

DEFINITIONS 97

Disclaimer

I make no claims that any of what's contained in this book will help you, your project, or your company. You are responsible for any losses or damages in any project, endeavor, or entity stemming from using any of the information contained in this book. This book explains how I manage documents in an Agile development environment, and it is only intended for that purpose.

What is a Gorilla?

If you're reading this book, I assume you know something about Agile and Scrum. You will also know the story of the chicken and the pig and how that stupid fable found its way into software development. Yeah that one: the chicken is involved, but the pig is committed. There's also the one about the rooster who struts around clucking worthless information and helping nobody. Well, let me tell you the fable of the chicken, the pig, the rooster, and the gorilla.

> *One day the pig, chicken, rooster, and gorilla were strolling down the road talking about opening a restaurant. The gorilla, however, was silent and said nothing as the conversation between the other three lasted for hours. Finally the three amigos realized the gorilla had not been saying anything the entire time. So they asked him, "Hey Gorilla? What do you think?" The gorilla looked down at them, grabbed the chicken and rooster by the neck in one hand, the pig in the other, lifted them off the ground, and said "Pig, you might be committed, Chicken, you might be involved, and Rooster, you're just talking nonsense, but all of you know this – I'm the one in charge."*

Be a Gorilla

Gorillas:

- Have a backbone (internal strength and conviction) and can make decisions and stick with them, even if others don't like those decisions.
- Have a take-charge attitude.
- Have thick skin.
- Take account for actions, both good and bad.
- Take account for what he/she produces, both good and bad.
- Love simplicity, not complexity.
- Are not necessarily sophisticated but intelligent.
- Plan well in advance.
- Avoid meetings after initial planning, unless absolutely necessary.
- Have a can-do attitude and are hard workers.
- Are not ones for BS and don't like to be told stories (falsehoods).
- Do not suffer fools well.
- Use foul language sometimes.
- Enjoy an occasional banana daiquiri.

Purpose

The number-one purpose of this book is to outline my process for producing decent-quality documents with the fewest assets, in the shortest time, while saving the maximum amount of money within an Agile project.

Am I a guru on this stuff? No. But I know what I know. And I'm a gorilla, so I'm going to tell what we gorillas do. Whether or not you swing through the documentation trees with me is up to you.

Although I have a master's degree, I'm not an academic, so there are no theories in this book. All my knowledge is based on past experience and trial and error. I didn't just make it up. There may be sections where you say, "Man, that ain't right!" Well for you, it might not be. For me it was and is.

What This Book Does

- Marries my document build-and-review process with the Agile SDLC and its processes
- Explains how my documents are managed as artifacts from a project manager's perspective, but developed from a tech writer's perspective
- Helps explain how I build lean-quality software documents within an Agile project
- Covers how I estimate, create, design, build, review, complete, and update, documents that accompany Agile—or some modified version of Agile—software development projects that I have either worked or consulted on
- Covers what I call "the document package" or "doc pack"— sometimes referred to as the "work package," "application package," "project package," or just "deliverables"
- Offers some estimation tools and cases from stories to pages to man-hours
- Contains workflow and document package Excel worksheets (12) through email after purchase.
- Uses some foul language and admonishes lots of innocent folks

What This Book is Not

A Writing Book

The actual writing, layout, and design of technical documents can be researched in a hundred other books. Additionally, many of those books offer design solutions, templates, and ideas for format (the arrangement of text, graphics, and other features on a page) for every conceivable type of document. My goal was not to write another book like that. This book concerns itself with the processes I use to create, build, review, and manage documents in an Agile project. However, there is a short section on writing conventions, philosophy, and style worth mentioning — at the end — should you be so inclined or want to impress your technical writer friends.

Long

You really want more shit to read? Grab yourself a copy of *War and Peace*, or worse, one of those wordy technical writing textbooks written by an academic who hasn't worked a day in the field. You have enough to do without reading a thick book on a dry subject that bores you to tears. Why should I make you reach for the hemlock? So no, it's not long — on purpose.

An Agile Documentation Book

Why? Because there is no such thing. That's why I don't use it in the title of this book. Most books on "Agile Documentation" seem to be nothing more than "Tech Writing 101" books. All the minimalistic documentation principles espoused in them were in existence long before Agile became a thought. These books simply steal from basic technical writing principles and call them "Agile." I looked at the original signatories of the Agile Manifesto; not one was a professional technical writer. I don't think documentation was a consideration outside of the "get rid of all of it" attitude when Agile was developed. The Agile methodology purports to do away with heavy documentation by stating, "Working software over comprehensive documentation." As if every waterfall project's goal is to produce mounds of documents. What is that?

And define "comprehensive" for me, would you? Or "just barely good enough?" What does that mean? I don't ever recall getting a paper back from my college writing professor with a grade of "just barely good enough." Nor do I ever remember turning over documents to a client saying, "Here, they're just barely good enough." Gorillas don't do "just barely good enough" work. We like to produce documents that get the job done well. While not overachievers, we look for value too. We are also accountable for our actions, both good and bad, and we understand that, if we're going to do something, we don't make a half-assed attempt. "Just barely good enough" documents may not *imply* low quality, but in reality, they are.

To me it sounds like "JBGE" is purposely ambiguous language designed to absolve the team of producing a quality document. That's simply because most developers and similar team members can't write or build documents properly. So they reduce the standard to accommodate this shortcoming and do away with technical writers.

Gorillas never sidestep responsibility. We are accountable for our actions and what we produce, both good and bad. If I couldn't write, I'd find somebody that could. I wouldn't lower the standards or do away with requirements just because I can't meet them. I always hear these software geeks say they need tech writers, but the processes they design and their actions speak otherwise.

So, there is Technical Writing and it ends there. It's up to you how you apply it. Any knucklehead claiming that Agile somehow invented a way to write must have way too many pens in his pocket protector.

A Help-You-Do-Everything Book

Twixt these pages I try to address everything I consider to be of value. All of this stuff was and is accurate for what I have done and am doing. However, it is not a be-all, end-all book for every conceivable need and scenario. Although the book delves into great detail in some sections, it is not an exhaustively comprehensive book on the subject, but more of a "highlights" outline. It assumes the reader has some knowledge of Agile and the documents associated with an Agile project.

Comparative Documentation Projects

Software documentation in an Agile project is generally small in scope by design. Although many documents may accompany an application, the number of people producing them is small — smaller than the number of people producing maintenance manuals for military aircraft, for example. These truly are projects unto themselves.

Aerospace Company Tech Pub Projects

Aerospace companies have entire publication departments dedicated to producing and maintaining military maintenance manuals. The projects are complete with directors, project managers, supervisors, admins, senior technical writers, technical editors, technical graphic artists, validators, SMEs, and so on. Their build philosophy and *modus operandi* are very different as well. Aerospace companies are very serious about quality and precise documentation, because if a step or specification in a maintenance manual is wrong, it could get somebody killed. While the writing is fair, the technical accuracy is spot-on. Everything is checked, double-checked, validated, and tested. Trust me, they do not fuck around.

Agile Projects

Agile software development projects, on the other hand, have technical writers *attached* to support a particular project and report directly to the project manager (PM here forward). The same is true in my current job. PMs, bless their hearts, are usually IT people with a computer science, database, or requirements analyst background who know little about documentation and the process it takes to build quality documents. Always on a time and money crunch with constant pressure to deliver a usable application, PMs look for a way to reduce the amount of documentation they deliver. While this is not a bad thing, they usually end up reducing quality. And that *is* a bad thing.

I am not—and would never want to be—a software development PM. I am, however, a lead on documentation projects and a full-time gorilla. I've had to learn many things an IT PM has to know, yet I've scarcely seen a PM do the same with my profession.

Why Use Professional Technical Writers?

Why do we have janitors? Perhaps we should have the project team clean the building? Pick a duty section each day, have them get mops, brooms, garbage bags, and get cracking. The same can be said for admins. Why do directors and program managers have them? Because no business wants their eighty-dollars-an-hour employees spending half the day sending out meeting invites and handling low-level bullshit.

PMs may think they're saving money by having the team produce the documents, and this may be true if they're producing few documents and a low page count. However that's rare. The reality is that it actually *costs* them money — and quality — by *not* having technical writers.

Producing documents, in an Agile context, is not a priority — it is a requirement. It's also not the sexiest thing to do. Most people, especially development teams, hate producing documents, and I don't blame them. If I have an MBA or an MS in computer science, the last thing I want to do is give birth to a wagon full of paper. I'd rather be doing what I was hired for and just supervise someone else doing it.

Top Eight Reasons (Not All-Inclusive)

- Technical people most often are not only poor writers but are usually the cause of the bulky documentation they rail against.
- It's cost effective. Would a company really want its seventy-dollars-an-hour people doing thirty-five-dollars-an-hour work?
- It is a division of labor. Technical writers are professionals dedicated to their craft and any project's documentation needs.

- Tech writers can do much of the heavy lifting of documents with a minimal amount of input from higher paid and more critical assets.
- Nobody wants to do documentation—especially developers, architects, and PMs.
- Writing documents takes away time from other team members' primary responsibilities.
- Without tech writers, your highly-paid and highly-skilled team will build clunky, overweight documents that are expensive and unusable.
- Tech writers are fun to be around.

Okay, maybe not the last one . . . . Well not me anyway. I'm a snarly, scar-faced, old gorilla with a disposition that makes the Wolverine look like Mother Theresa. Just sayin'. . . .

And lastly, according the bureau of labor and statistics, there are some 50,000 people that list their profession as a technical writer. Why can't all these people, PhDs and the like, be smart enough to realize they are not needed? Poor buggers. Unlike some disciplines that have been on the decline and become obsolete, technical writing has gone in the other direction. It has emerged out of necessity over the years in response to the demands of the information age. And the demand only seems to be growing.

Minimalism Saves Money

Gorillas like to save money and not waste time; that's why we like minimalism. You can google the term "minimalism" in all its forms: art, architecture, interior design, music, and of course, literature. For me, minimalism, as applied to the contents of the document, is tactical. Sometimes this is referred to as "lean writing" or "lean documentation." *Strategic* refers to the contents of the document package. *Strategic* is covered in the "Data-Slim the Doc Pack" section of this book. *Tactical* is covered in the "Writing: Conventions, Philosophy, and Style" section.

Tactical Minimalism

Applied tactical minimalism pares documents down to their most utilitarian form. It requires only the text it takes to get the job done. At the sentence level, it is devoid of any unnecessary adjectives and words that don't add value; at the paragraph level, it is devoid of any sentences that don't add value; etc., etc., up to the section/chapter level. In addition, my text/graphics split is about 70/30.

Tactical minimalism makes the writing a bit choppy and terse to the literary sect, but it builds documents that fit all the requirements of an Agile software project: cheap, fast, accurate, and simple.

Strategic Minimalism

Strategic minimalism is important because very few document teams actually take the time to (or even know how to) efficiently reduce redundancies and overlaps across and within the document package. This type of minimalism doesn't concern itself with writing, but more reducing redundant data between documents that has been written or is projected to be written. Strategic minimalism also involves removing entire documents. Gorillas always make sure this happens; just ask the chicken and the pig.

Culprits

On the tactical level, many authors love to write documents ornate with colorful adjectives, metaphors, literary references, and other fluff to make them seem more "authorial." It's simply unnecessary. Developers? *Notorious* for overwritten documents. Engineers as well. "Throw enough shit at the page and see what sticks" seems to be an axiom. If it weren't for them, I'd be out of a job.

On the strategic level, many bureaucrats love their documents and are leery of getting rid of them. They fear it leaves too many oversight gaps for the project. They also want the team punching the right holes and think that producing a bunch of documents is the way to do it. And then there are documents that pertain to (and are sometimes generated by) a particular entity/organization. They fear if their documents are taken away, they might become irrelevant — or worse yet — out of a job. I disagree of course, but that has been my experience with both public and private sectors.

That in mind, gorillas enforce a minimalist or lean philosophy in the document crew — whoever they are: tech writers, developers, engineers, BAs, tech editors, etc. It's crucial to have the most muscular writing methods when producing informational documents.

Prior to project kickoff, I usually give a one-to-two-hour long work session/seminar/class on tactical minimalism (i.e., lean writing). That way, all the authors understand what's expected (well close anyway). And of course, "Data-Slim the Doc Pack."

Therefore . . .

Gorillas write tight, write less, and use the fewest amount of documents they can get away with.

No unnecessary
- Words in a sentence.
- Sentences in a paragraph.
- Paragraphs in a section.
- Sections in a document.
- Documents in the document package.

And I mean not *one*. Not one single, unnecessary anything. Strict enforcement of this rule pays off. The documents will be shorter by at least 20–30 percent.

This translates into decreased
- Creation times.
- Build times.
- Review times.
- Update times.
- Management difficulty.
- Storage space (if this is a concern).

Wasted man-hours creating fat, clunky, overwritten documents is the hidden leviathan of so many organizations, especially large ones. I can't even tell you. Gorillas minimalize, my friend, both tactically and strategically.

Replacing Text with Graphics

Gorillas like lots of pictures, but replacing text with graphics wherever possible doesn't fit every scenario, especially when it comes to documents like the user and installation guides. Although this is a useful technique employed by technical writers, problems can happen.

The author may, for example, have trouble acquiring the graphics. And graphics can be difficult to manage depending on the project. I've worked on projects where I didn't have access to the test environment, and the development team wasn't exactly *mach schnell* with the screenshots. Sometimes it's quicker to write it out. A picture is worth a thousand words? Maybe, but I only use them when necessary, *not* just to replace text that I'm too lazy to write.

Also, if there are different deployment sites for the application, the screens may not look the same. The screenshots used from the test environment may or may not match the deployment sites, as they may be configured differently. This situation happens a lot in the manufacturing industry. And any information that is updated must be site-specific for the same reason. So, in this instance, more text is better, because it is universal.

Additionally, the file size of your final product might be an issue. And those graphics have to load into your browser or application. Lots of graphics to load takes time and they might become unstable. Lots of graphics can make response times slow — especially if your published output format is Word. So gorillas always consider the text-graphics split when creating documents, particularly user-facing documents.

Considerations

- Document size (may affect load times and storage space)
- Screenshot sources (will they be readily accessible to the author?)
- Configuration (if deployed to multiple sites, are they configured similarly?)
- Clarity (some formats don't transfer or print well)
- Document updates (harder than changing text and they need to match other sites)

A Case Study . . . of a Sort

During the last few years, while working at a number of contracts and with a number of consults, I applied lean writing principles to numerous documents, including user guides and design documents. I took my edits and rewritten documents and gave presentations to various directors, managers, leads, and so forth. I showed them all the waste that was going on right under their noses.

On average, I decreased the size of the document by 30 percent. Most of the content that got slashed was unnecessary, superfluous, nice to know but irrelevant, or simply in the wrong place. The reaction from the audience was always the same . . . silence.

I remember one particular company. . . .

"That 900-page user guide you gave me I took 6 pages and cut them down to 4. That's a 33-percent reduction. If that were true for the whole guide that would mean roughly 300 hundred pages are worthless. That's not only a savings of 300 pages, *but* also all the work that goes with them. If you use the formula I showed you for creating and reviewing this doc, that's about 5 man-hours per each page X 300, which equals 1500 man-hours wasted. 1500! *And* you let your seventy-dollars-an-hour developer write it so that's at least two man-hours of the formula (including updates, changes, and new material) so that's 600 man-hours X $70, which equals $42,500. Not to mention being taken away from his or her primary responsibility, which is coding. So that's lost time as well that I don't have a metric for.

There's also your thirty-five-dollars-an-hour tech writer that wasted two hours per page (including updates, changes, and comment incorporation, but mostly edits), so that's 600 X $35, which equals $21,000.

And last but not least, the person who did the tech edit was probably another developer/BA at sixty dollars per hour. So let's just say, 300 X $60/hr = $18,000.

So you just wasted, um, roughly, $81, 500 on *one* doc . . . .

It's got nice front matter though . . . .

The font is pretty nice too . . . .

So, hey is there a café in the building?"

They all stared at me. Apparently, gorilla sarcasm wasn't on the menu that day. Ah well; didn't affect my paycheck.

If they would have had their technical writer help write the documentation instead of just edit it, he/she could have taken much of the burden off of the developer, thus saving money. The writing would have been much tighter, and the waste would have been much less. The company also brought the tech writer into the project late, which may have saved a little money. But, had the tech writer been there at inception, my guess is that the tech writer could have written the majority of the guide, making developer participation minimal. Additionally, lean writing would have decreased pagination, which, as I stated previously, has a domino effect on saving money.

Even if I was off by half in my estimation, that's still forty grand wasted for one user guide. Apply that to a whole doc pack consisting of fifty documents (the government agencies I consulted for often had seventy or more) and you'll see that the waste on overweight documents is ridiculous.

Take away: Less means more. More money, more time. So write less, but write efficiently.

Order of Concerns Paradigm

Should I need to hire, pick, or at least screen the tech writer(s) and/or editor(s) assigned to the project, there are a few things I look for. Technical writers and editors are going to hate me for this section. But hey, if baby is ugly. . . .

Before I address the differences, take a look at the "Order of Concerns" paradigm for writing. You'll see why in a minute. Different organizations use different paradigms but this is what I use. Gorillas love a sense of order.

The Four Higher-Order Concerns

- Audience
    - Who you are writing to (determines content, style, reading level)
- Content
    - The information contained in any communiqué
- Organization
    - The organization of the content (simple to complex, most important to least, chronological, etc.,) within the document or paragraph
- Format
    - The organization of the content (text, graphics, and other devices) on a page
    - Output format, such as PDF, HTML Help, Web Help, etc.

The Four Lower-Order Concerns

- Mechanics
    - The way a sentence is constructed
- Word Choice
    - The words in a sentence chosen to convey proper meaning
- Grammar
    - The rules that govern sentence construction
- Spelling and Punctuation

Technical Editors

Ernest Hemingway, who to me is Papa Gorilla, is someone I admire. It wasn't just the way he wrote, it was the way he lived. He took a big bite out of life and checked out on his own terms. But as great as he was, he didn't edit his own stuff. His editor was Maxwell Perkins. Perkins also edited for F. Scott Fitzgerald and Thomas Wolfe. So, if three of our greatest writers needed editors, chances are you do too. And if you need them, it's important to know what they do. Remember, we are addressing technical editors, not editors from a newspaper or publishing house. Also, see the section on "Technical Edits." In no particular order:

Responsibilities

- *Not* technical edits
- Lower-order concerns
- Copy edits (including format edits)
- Output edits (from a multi-channel authoring system)
- Fact-checks / validations, if qualified
- Middle- or end-of-the document build processes
- Rules and correctness of sentence structure
- Keen attention to detail, systematic, organized
- Enforces style considerations and standards
- Not necessarily a gorilla (although I have seen some with hair on their knuckles)

Background

- English, communication, or journalism (prose, literature, grammar, writing)

Technical editors are usually not involved with the creation of content but rather the manipulation of existing content within the context of the lower order concerns. They also do format edits but are not involved in the design phase. They can be brought in to consult on any levels of concern and can create content, but it's best to have them dedicated to their specialty.

Editing Metrics

Technical editors are employed to complete different levels of editing. Below is my list of editing metrics:
- Developmental (1–1.5 pages per hour)
- Substantive (2 pages per hour)
- Copy edit (3–4 pages per hour)
- Proofread (5–7 pages per hour)

Different entities have their recommendations, which are slightly different than what I use, but you can google "editing services" to get an idea.

The metrics in the above bullets are for general documents. So they *will not* match what is outlined in the "Planning and Estimating Tools" section. Past experience has shown me that user and installation guides do not fit this metric very well.

In light of those four types of edits, I consider only two: technical and copy (a business edit would fall under technical).

See the table below:

Type of Edit	Concerns	Need Subject Matter Knowledge
Technical	Higher	Yes
Copy edit	Lower	No

People in the IT field, especially developers, think of technical writing as being synonymous with editing. It's not. The truth is, some people are good at just creating stuff, but need someone to polish it. Conversely, some people can't create anything, but can turn "Jabberwocky" into Shakespeare. That's usually the case of a good editor.

Good editors are hard to find, and — from what I've seen — the talent is innate. They're different from writers in a few ways. This is not to say they can't write, but in my opinion, they have a special eye for detail and see things most others do not.

Additionally, they are very knowledgeable in the ways of grammar and usually come from a literary or journalism background. And they have at least one grammar, comparative grammar, or rhetorical grammar class under their belt.

Why One Dedicated Editor is Optimal

On any project, having a dedicated tech editor is optimal, or at least one writer dedicated to editing. Why? Focus, mindset, workload, and a fresh set of eyes. It's also where bang meets buck. And you know gorillas love value. Decent quality; fewest assets.

Focus

Good editors are systematic. When they edit a document, they do so with the fewest amount of priorities in one pass. For example, an editor might start off with a format edit to make sure all the text, graphics, and other devices are arranged properly on the page. Or, if he/she is qualified, he/she may do some fact-checking or validate steps in the test environment of the application. The next pass on the document may be a voice check. The next pass might be grammar or vice versa. Or simply a copy edit. Each pass requires a different focus, which in turn increases quality. Some editors do this all at once, but I think it's not as efficient. If my project has at least one dedicated editor, I know we will have decent-quality documents.

A Fresh Set of Eyes

After the document is written, it should be sent to a technical editor to get a fresh set of eyes looking at it. It will be something he/she has never seen before. That way, all the mistakes that everyone has overlooked will now become apparent. This is true with anyone really. When a person looks at the document they've written over and over again, they don't see the mistakes anymore. It's true you can "put it down for a couple days" and have a fresh set of eyes, but in an Agile environment, you don't have that luxury.

Mindset

It takes a different type of intellectual energy and a different degree of concentration to edit documents as opposed to creating them. If your technical editor has only one mindset, the quality of the document goes up as does the efficiency of the edit. Though most editors can multitask, intellectually it's not good practice. The same is true for technical writers.

Workload

If I have two technical writers on a project, it's okay, because they can alternate what they edit and handle a heavier workload. Ideally I like to have at least a technical writer and a technical editor, as I said earlier. If there is only one technical writer that is doing all the copy editing as well as creating his/her assigned documents, it's really not a good system. It's also trying to get by on the cheap. I know; money, money, money, I get it. But quality improves as well as CBC (create, build, complete) times if there are two people working on documents. If I don't have two technical writers, I try to get the PM to secure an asset, such as an editor or another technical writer part-time so they can do some copy editing for the project.

If All Else Fails

If one of my projects is in a money crunch and I'm the only technical writer attached, I implore the PM to scan the project management application and see if he/she can steal some hours from some of our do-nothings in the crew — or even me — and give those hours to either another technical writer or tech editor. We use a bill number with a set amount of hours, and work it out ahead of time. The best time to use our newly-stolen asset is at output just before delivery time. We have him/her do a one-pass output edit on the documents that concern us most, and then I incorporate the comments. It's not the best way of doing things, but if nothing else, it affords us another level of QA.

Technical Writers

The kings of documentation ... uh hem ....

The responsibilities and backgrounds of technical writers and technical editors are different. A technical writer's job can include either creating content or aiding in the creation thereof. Technical writers can function as editors, but it is not their primary duty. Their most important function is the *delivery* of that content. They surmise the best way to communicate the content and work with the author/SME to do so.

Technical writers in the software field usually have a background — or considerable experience in — IT. If I am on the hiring board for interviewing technical writers, I look for the following experience in their background:

Background

- Degree in technical or professional writing
- Structure and organization of documents, brevity, minimalism
- Rhetoric and argument
- Heavy concern with content delivery through information structuring (hierarchy of chunks, labelling, integrating graphics, relevance), formatting, and reusing capabilities (tagging, metadata)
- Experience in IT, engineering, or the field they write in (at least one coding class, Java, C++, info systems training)
- Familiarity with the OASIS Language standard and DITA
- Familiarity with building and/or employing IETMs
- Languages: XML, XHTML, XSLT, HTML, and use of / creation of DTDs or schemas
- Modular writing, information mapping, seven Infotypes
- Technical documentation applications such as MadCap Flare, RoboHelp, Arbortext, FrameMaker, XMetaL, Stylus Studio, *and* Oxygen
- Familiarity with CMSs such as Astoria, Vasont, Documentum, and yes, SharePoint
- Some training or experience in eliciting, gathering, and producing requirements (Value Stories, Epics, Stories) and features
- Training in, or at least understanding of Information Architecture and User Research
- Some API stuff

Duties

- Tasked with document development from the very beginning of the build process
- Tasked with higher order concerns and producing personas
- Work closely and heavily with SMEs and sometimes become them
- Create, build, complete, manage, and maintain assigned documents
- Support the project as a whole
- Create and enforce uniformity standards for your documents (along with the editor)
- Create and execute a workflow for specified documents
- Serve as an asset to the development team
- Copy edit , when assigned, other documents from other projects
- Complete technical edits, if qualified
- Raid the coffee bar
- Cry about getting no respect

What They Are Not

- Editing squad (as in only)
- Scribes
- Admins
- Secretaries
- Graphic designers
- Literary creators
- Novelists
- Coders
- And my biggest source of irritation—**meeting minute takers** (I mean *beyond* irritated)

A Word on Faux Tech Writers

Many aerospace corporations hire ex-military personnel, such as mechanics, electronic technicians, pilots, etc., as technical writers to update and maintain maintenance manuals for aircraft and vehicles. These companies get away with it because the manuals are already built, and the structure is so strict due to DTDs and templates, so all these writers have to do is learn Arbortext and fill in content. I was a part of a number of these projects, and I'm sorry, but I don't consider them real technical writers. If one of these "technical writers" were ever taken out of their structured bubble, they'd be lost. Most are simply SMEs with a keyboard. They know the material well and are very concerned with technical correctness and safety, but I don't recall any of them ever having anything in the writing field above a high school grammar or one college writing class. I know, I'm a snob right? Tough.

So, when many companies want to hire a technical writer, quite often they look for a person with an SME background. These companies go on the cheap and want to kill two birds with one stone. This works fine in the above-listed scenario. But when these SMEs have no technical writer for reference and are tasked with creating everything from scratch, the result is a disaster. The organization and structure of the documents are the biggest victims followed by features of the doc and sentence structure. Minimalism? A phantom.

I have come across software development companies doing the same thing. They'll ask for a technical writer with a programming background, like in Java or .net. What *experienced* programmer wants to write documents when he/she can make more money as a coder? It's nonsense. I know they exist, but in twenty years of this business (eight in software development), I met *one*. Here's what happens: The company finds a junior coder that needs a job then have him/her write the docs. And they come out like shit. Smart kids usually, as I have known a few, but they write the documents as though the system is talking to itself. WTF? Not a clue; not one damn clue. But I don't blame them; they weren't trained for it. I blame the entity that hired them in the first place.

The other source of consternation I have is with editors that claim to be technical writers. In the DC area, the average editor makes about fifty grand, and the average tech writer makes about seventy. Quite often, these editors have some technical writing experience but only from the lower order of concerns level. So they re-invent themselves as a technical writer and ride the bullshit train to a higher paying position. But once hired, they simply can't do the job. They function well as editors but need to be trained on the technical things they should already know. I have experienced this more than once. Get hired, work with the team and other "tech writers" only to find out that their solutions are not only dated but based in the literary field.

I can always tell their background when one of them says to me they've worked only in *Word* and not a multi-channel authoring system or an XML based system. The other sign is their style of writ: beautiful prose that's too clunky for IT docs. I respect editors a lot. I suck at editing. My gorilla grammar has always been suspect, but gorillas don't bullshit. Don't tell me a story and say you're something you're not. Especially when you're at my desk every five minutes asking me shit you should already know — and you get paid the same amount of bananas as me.

Perhaps I'm wrong. Maybe anybody can be a technical writer. They trained elephants to paint right? Hell, maybe I should train my dog how to hold a pen and send his ass to work. Maybe buy a donkey, give him an easel board and a piece of chalk and see if he can draw a flowchart. . . .

Okay, enough ranting. Next up. . . .

Technical Edits: The Subject Matter Expert (SME)

Technical edits, by my definition, are not conducted by a technical editor. Sounds strange right? A technical editor is an editor who edits technical material. This person may or may not have subject matter knowledge and therefore may or may not be altering the technical validity of the document.

A **technical edit** must be done by someone who has a thorough knowledge of the application or subject. This person, known as a Subject Matter Expert (SME), determines the technical validity of the material and nothing else. An SME rarely has an editorial background and can be a PM, business/requirements analyst, development lead, application architect, or someone of the sort.

A technical edit can also be conducted by someone who is efficient at — and has the time and resources for — either fact-checking or validation. This takes too long, though, so it's best to have someone who knows the information right off the top of their head or can get it quickly.

Technical Writer as SME

For technical writers to have subject matter knowledge, they need to be included in any application design, requirements, and build meetings from the onset of the project—meaning inception or planning—and certainly when the first sprint starts through deployment. As the project progresses, many times the technical writers *become* SMEs. Additionally, on many projects, technical writers are required to maintain certain documents even after the project is delivered. So having them involved often and early is optimal. Doing so also reduces the need for technical support from an SME to build or update a document.

Spreadsheets Email

You've reached the point where you need the spreadsheets. They will help you understand my process. To obtain your excel spreadsheet with the 12 tabs, email me at arealgorillasguide@gmail.com . Be sure to include your product ID number inside the back page. You should have them within a few hours.

Build Documents-the Gorilla Way

If I'm going to build documents, it would be nice to know which ones I have to build. So the first thing I do is . . .

Determine the Doc Pack

To kick off the document planning stage, as it were, gorillas like to have the PM (hopefully another gorilla) hold a doc pack meeting for the entire project team. Some orgs call it optimization, initial planning, work package meeting . . . . Whatever anyone calls the meeting where the documents are determined—that's what I'm talking about.

The first thing in the doc pack meeting that needs to be determined is which documents will be created for the project. The project team should go over the list of required and optional documents, as well as others that may be necessary. All team members should have at least some input, including stakeholders, if feasible.

Most of the time, I fight to keep only the documents necessary. I also try to opt out the required documents, especially if there are only certain sections that are needed. From experience, I can sometimes gauge which document these sections can be integrated into, and I push for that. I have a slash-and-burn mentality when it comes to determining the doc pack. If there is any doubt about keeping a document, then it is excluded. If the project has a lot of oversight, though, I am usually stuck with a huge doc pack, whether I like it or not.

Projects differ and the content of the doc pack changes with each one. But if I had my way? The doc pack would consist of the following documents: the Technical Design Document, which would include the SDD and ADD; the Project Plan, which includes the schedule; the Install Plan; Deploy Plan; User Guide; Installation Guide; and maybe a Test Approach and Security Plan or report. The rest can be handled by the RMS.

Once the contents of the doc pack have been determined, the next step is to assign authors.

Assign Authors

The best way, in my opinion, to maximize control and minimize confusion is for each particular document to have only *one* designated author—top gorilla—for the document. That person is responsible for the document until responsibility is transferred. That responsibility includes supervising the build. The author may have others contributing data to the doc. They may be SMEs, peers, other authors, or technical personnel. But each contributor is *not* considered the author of that document.

Author's Duties:

- Is a gorilla
- Is wholly responsible for the document (under the PM)
- Is an SME on the document's contents
- Is a member of the authorial team
- Decides how to build the doc (in conference with the tech writer)
- Helps decide the best organizational schema
- Assigns sections to the authorial team
- Decides when to initiate reviews
- Controls the frequency of data intake and updates
- Does *not* perform the technical edit on his/her writing (done by peer(s) with equal knowledge)

Assign Authorial Teams and Other Roles

Once the authors have been assigned, the authorial team needs to be decided. The key is to assign the contributors to documents with authors that have the same or similar skillsets as that contributor—hence the term peer. A peer is not just anyone, but rather is someone who has at least some subject matter knowledge for the document they are contributing to. The author, of course, should be the top SME.

The PM should have complete control of these assignments, as they are his/her assets. An author might want five people working on his/her document, but perhaps only two can be spared. The PM will have to make that call.

The same goes for all other assignments, such as copy edits, tech edits, and sign-offs. Filling out the People Tracker spreadsheet helps give the PM an accurate picture of the workload. It's best to work this out with everyone present; that way, any debating or people-shuffling can take place in the open. So, if anybody has a gripe, they can voice it.

Authorial Team Size

Gorillas don't like too many hands peeling the same banana. So, when it comes to building documents, more is not better. Having a large authorial team for any particular document can actually expand CBC times. The more people involved, the longer it takes. Some might think that CBC times would decrease if more people were on the team doing work, but an overload point exists. Too many competing opinions and comments spawn arguments that last forever and slow the build process. It's key to find the balance between workload, assets, and efficiency.

I like to have at least two SMEs building a document—one the author, the other a contributor. They do technical edits on each other's work. If there is more than one contributor, it's best to have an author who is a gorilla. That way, he/she can keep a lid on any squabbling that may occur during the build and keep the process on track. If the tech writer is the author, then an SME does the tech edit and an editor does the copy edit.

I know writers always say that building documents is a collaborative effort—true—but having one strong person in charge of that collaboration is crucial. If not, the document's direction may be all over the map. I learned as a director on several short films that it's a bitch to solve things by committee, especially amongst creative types. Same thing happened to me on one particular development project, but I wasn't the lead. The people in charge had no backbone. It was a horror show. So I like *one* person in charge of each document, and he/she better be a gorilla.

Once all personnel have been assigned, the team goes through the entire document package and completes the Doc Prep Checklist.

Complete the Doc Prep Checklist

AKA: Requirements Capture for the Documents

Gorillas like to plan, so the next thing that needs be done is for authors to complete the Doc Prep Checklist. This can be conducted all together or during individual meetings for each document. I believe it's best to have all authors, authorial teams, the product owner, and the business owner, if possible. If these people aren't available, the checklist should be sent to them for buy-in. Like I say on the spreadsheet, it's a cover-your-ass list. A gorilla never goes down a road without key stakeholders on board, especially if they have to build an extensive and crucial user guide. I don't want to end up three days before delivery with the business owner saying, "That's not the organization I wanted," or "I wanted more features." You got requirements for the application right? Well secure the requirements for the documents too.

Now the team is ready for . . .

The Gorilla Build/Review Process

Gorillas are process-oriented and they don't like "wingin' shit." The following section is an outline I use to build, review, and complete documents. The Build Review/Process consists of two parts: the Doc Prep Checklist and the Build/Review Cycle (BRC or "brick"). All of these are outlined in the spreadsheets that accompany the book. Review them before going forward.

The Build/Review Process (BRP) can be started and completed within any phase, depending on the document, or it can run through all phases. For example, a Project Management Plan may need to be created, built, and completed within the plan, the initiate, or even the concept phase, if it's considered a "green-light" doc. By contrast, the user guide might be created in the plan phase and completed in the execution/development phase just prior to deployment, or in between or across several milestones. The user guide may also be created during the testing period and completed in time for deployment. The build process doesn't necessarily have to parallel or intersect any specific time period, whether it be sprints, milestones, or phases, unless it is designed that way.

Also, the team can create all documents in the package in the initiate phase once the doc prep checklist has been finished. That way, all the docs are ready for build throughout all phases of the project. With a small doc pack, this seems to work fine. With a large one, though, it may be too much.

In an Agile project, gorillas build documents in small, usable, chunks (i.e., topics), just like you do with the application.

Numbers 0.0–7.0 are the steps of the Doc Prep Checklist. They can be completed in twenty minutes or two weeks, depending on the project. They are the invisible part of the build, but crucial nonetheless.

The Doc Prep Checklist

0.0 Do I Need to Create It?

- Is it required? Needed?
- Is the information covered in another document? If so, can that be used and/or integrated?
    - This is an initial analysis. Comprehensive analysis is conducted in "Data-Slim the Doc Pack".
- Need should be covered in document package meeting, but can be revisited.
- If a template exists, steps 1–7 may not be needed. But I go through them anyway to make sure the template accommodates the project needs.

1.0 Perform Audience Analysis

- Who is going to use it or read it?
- What persona is needed?
- What level? (Coleman-Liau index, Flesch-Kincaid Grade Level, ARI (Automated Readability Index), SMOG. To access these indexes, google the free online tool.

2.0 Decide Purpose or Intent

The two types of intent I use are:
- Inform
    - **Example of inform**: "Company technicians will maintain the servers."
- Persuade
    - **Example of persuade**: "Our experienced team of competent technicians will consistently maintain your high-speed servers on a twenty-four-hour basis."

Purpose or intent will have an impact on organization, structure, and sentence mechanics. Informational documents are simple and straightforward (subject, verb, and object). Persuasion documents use different modes and devices and usually more adjectives.

Persuasion can be from the sentence level, as in the example given above (ethos), to the level of the entire document. To get a better idea of persuasion techniques, google "modes of persuasion" or "rhetorical strategies".

3.0 Decide the Type of Document

There are seven different information types, as per Robert Horn, but I use the DITA types. Most of Horn's information types fall into these three categories anyway.

- Concept: Theory of ops, exposition type, description of something, paragraph form
- Task: To do something, steps, second person imperative
- Reference: Tables, charts, definitions, parts manuals, etc.

4.0 Decide the Organizational Schema

These schemas can be mixed. For example, an SDD may be organized according to functions, and those functions may in turn may be organized chronologically (reflecting when they were built — which to me is stupid — but I have seen this), or they may be organized from biggest to smallest.

A list of organizational schemas is below:

- Process (business processes, R&R procedures): the order in which a task is done
- Spatial (e.g., as per tab arrangement) common in user guides
- Chronological (usually related to time; different from process)
- Grouped (usually based on functions or features)

- Simple to complex, or vice versa (systems and subsystems descriptions)
- Most important to least important (can be based on business processes)
- Most-used to least-used (process- or task-related)
- Workflow (assembly line)
- Direct (big idea followed by support)
- Indirect (evidence first, big idea toward the end)

The last two are usually for argument or business documents. Sometimes in parts of proposals.

5.0 Determine the Document Output Format

It's crucial for the business and product owner to buy off on the output format. If the team has multi-channel publishing software, it doesn't matter too much, unless the document has lots of features. But with only Word, the technical writer may need a PDF exchange or plug in, or if the client/owner wants online output he/she will need extra time to import and edit. If the client wants context-sensitive help (CSH) the team will definitely need the appropriate authoring software.

The list below addresses some output format questions:

- What type of format works best for the needs of the target audience? Word, PDF, HTML help, Web help, HTML5 help, .NET help, mobile?
- What type fits best with the application?
- Will the selected output have one file with embedded images (Word, PDF, HTML help) or multiple files with referenced images and files (Web help, HTML5 help, etc.)?
- What are the update capabilities of the new owner of the documents?

- Who will update them after deployment? Ops, new owner, client, etc., and do they have the capability to update the documents with the chosen format?
- Will help be embedded or at one locale? (Usually a development decision.)

6.0 Determine Types of Devices
Will the documents have?

- Navigation devices?
- Index, glossary?
- Text, graphics, tables, smart diagrams, videos, etc.?
- Hyperlinks, xrefs, Skin Buttons?
- Bubbles, popups, collapsible text, dropdowns, etc.?
- Context-Sensitive Help (CSH)? (Crucial for user guides.)

7.0 Determine the Best Sources to Aid Document Build
Data to build documents can come from:

- Requirements management software (ALM, TFS, Rational, Rally Agile Designer, whatever your flavor;) (read the updates by developers and determine impacted documents then incorporate changes)
- SME
- Development team
- Supporting documents (list them for each document)

Where the authorial team should get information from if not an SME:
- Example: User guide sources for the tech writer might be user acceptance testing, acceptance criteria, the requirements analyst, or the developer. The flow might be Code > features > documented by developer > updates in requirement management software > tech writer turns into tasks.

NOTE: It's best to have the tech writer on the project from the beginning so he/she will know the application. If not, having heavy support from the SME is necessary.

End Doc Prep Checklist.

Now you're ready to rock and review. . . .

The Build/Review Cycle (BRC)

8.0 Create the Document

- Complete the Doc Prep Checklist.
- Determine sections to be written and frame up the document (think in terms of blocks, modules, chunks, or topics).
- Build the table of contents by using placeholder titles.

- Use first-level headers for sections, second-level headers for subsections, third-level headers for tasks (usually).
- Create the cover, front matter, header, footer, etc.
- Design the layout.
- Determine how all the text, graphics, tables, glossary, index, and every device (dropdowns, collapsible text, hyperlinks, cross references, xrefs) that will appear on the page will look.
- Complete the template.
- Place the document in the proper directory. (From here forward, "One document, one author, one place, always." No copies anywhere else are considered valid. Everyone works on the same doc that sits in the same place, and it doesn't move until designated by the PM.)
- Get the "okay", buy-in, concurrence, or signatures (if necessary) on the framework.
- Lock the doc (read only) if it's not ready to open (though the doc should be closed at this point).
- Annotate in the document package summary or some other tracking device that it has been created (if necessary).
- Add the created document to the workflow (if necessary) Excel for paper, or create electronic in CMS.
- Data-slim the doc pack. (Not true part of BRC but is completed after document is created)

9.0 Open the Document

- Unlock for data input (done by author, tech writer, or PM).
- Notify designated personnel (this may be the whole team or just those assigned to build the document) by email or other communication.
- Turn on Track Changes (if it's a Word document) or some tracking device for whatever authoring software is being used.
    - It is possible to wait until the original build is finished and just use Track Changes for updates. However this, along with the workflow, can help identify who is doing what, how

often, and when—as well as what—the original information was and what the updates are.
  - If you don't care about this step, skip it, but at least turn on the Track Changes.

10.0 Build the Document

- Input data as it becomes available (as determined by the sources for the document in step 7.0;) (done by the author and authorial team).
- Build in small, manageable chunks or topics (google "modular and topic-based writing").
- Run the workflow at pre-designated times or when appropriate.

11.0 Review the Document

- Follow the workflow as per assigned roles and responsibilities.
- Conduct *mini* reviews at any time
- Conduct the *final* review two weeks prior to delivery (optimally, but five business days is common. Or you can do the final review in the UAT period, if you are running a mixed model).
- Close or lock the document if it is in the final review stage.
- Complete the copy edit and ensure all comments have been adjudicated, then send the document to sign-off (done by the tech writer in the final review if sign-off is necessary).

12.0 Sign-off (if required; if sign-off is not required, go to step 13.0)

- The sign-off person reviews the document in its entirety for everything.
- Sign-off is completed in the final review.
- Signature flow is sometimes necessary (see "Large BRC" in the spreadsheets included with this book).

- Major comments made by the sign-off person adjudicated by document status being changed to the appropriate person in workflow.
- Minor comments from the sign-off person are cleared by email, phone call, or other means.
- The document is sent to the technical writer for completion, once the sign-off person is satisfied with it.

13.0 Complete Document (done in *final* review)

A completed document:

- Has been signed off (if necessary).
- Has no outstanding comments from any stage in the workflow.
- Has received a final copy edit (if published format is in Word).
- Has received validation (e.g., user guide procedures) (should have been included in the final review cycle if determined necessary).
- Has already been through the final review cycle (including a business edit, if necessary).
- Receives a final output edit (if publishing to multiple formats).
- Has been versioned.
- Has been readied for transfer to the new owner, etc. (if being delivered).
- Has been included as part of a document package zip file (if necessary).
- Has been included as part of the complete document package if the online package was requested.

Data-Slim the Doc Pack

Gorillas love cutting fat, so we love data-slim. Although it is not part of the BRC, data-slim is part of step 8.0 of the BRC and should be conducted between the creation and build phases. This process is a great way to minimalize the number and size of documents in the package.

Data-slim requires a meeting with all authorial teams present. The team openly compares data or projected data across all documents in the package. Almost invariably, there is information — even entire documents — that can be cut, merged, or incorporated.

This process absolutely reduces any possible redundancies. Sometimes one document can be incorporated into another.

Gorillas' Data-Slim Steps

1. Build the structure of the docs in the pack down to the topic level (completed in step 8.0 of the BRC before data-slim meeting) which is usually third- and fourth-level headers.
2. Have teams look for headers that are similar in the same document, as well as in different documents.
3. Have authorial teams converse about and compare whether projected data input will be the same.
4. Decide if any similar data can be integrated into one document or the other, or if one document could reference the other.
5. Determine if modules can be reused.

If data cannot be referenced and must be in both places, one team writes the topic and the other copies and pastes it into their document. Both teams do not write the exact same thing.

If there are two or three documents with the same headers and the same projected data input, I combine the info into one document and have the other documents reference it, or I use hyperlinks and xrefs from one document to the other. But gorillas don't write the same shit twice. Call us lazy, but hey. . . .

A good example is within a user guide that has to serve both users and admins, with both sections needing to be separate. Many times tasks and subtasks will be identical for the two roles. This is where an authoring system with online output capabilities is beneficial. The author simply writes the modules once and reuses them by dragging and dropping them in the table of contents (TOC) in both places.

Data-Slim Exceptions

Exceptions exist, though, such as in the user guide and training materials. Even though training is concept-based and user is task-based, much of these two kinds of materials will have redundant information. Connecting the two documents, however, reduces redundancy. Other documents I can think of would be the CONOPS and the PMP that the government uses. Tons of redundancy, but the documents are meant for different groups of people with totally different sign-off paths. Don't know if that's the best way but . . .

Gorilla Hopes for Data-Slim

If I can pare the whole doc pack down to six documents — whether at the doc pack meeting or during data-slim — I'm happy. And furthermore, if I can slim the docs I have down to the bare essentials, I'm happier yet. Many technical writers would think I'm killing job security — trust me; I'm not. The more docs in the package and the more data in the document, the more babysitting I have to do, and gorillas are horrible babysitters. Plus, if I have additional time due to a slimmed doc pack, I can be tasked out to help other projects or learn more about the application. I don't really enjoy sitting on my ass surfing the net all day. Nor do I care about who's sleeping with who at the office. I do, however, care if bananas are on the café's daily menu.

Fewer documents with leaner writing reduces man hours and cost. Even if I have a lousy author crew, data-slimming the doc pack cuts down on lots of work.

Once Development Starts

Remember, this is not a technical writing book. The layout and design of the actual documents can be researched in many other books.

Once development starts (i.e., sprints) I open all docs that have not already been opened, and add data to the assigned documents I am authoring as soon as I have information. I also encourage the PM to have the other authors do the same. I use the data-gathering method, people, and documents outlined at the meeting and add the information in small, manageable chunks or topics. I only document what the system actually does, not the speculative stuff.

The only exceptions are those documents that must be completed before development starts, such as an ADD, SDD, TAD, and others to get the project off the ground, but they get updated anyway.

Depending how my unit is set up, the authors (including me) get updates from the development group or the Requirements Management Software (RMS). This could be daily, every few days, or at the end of the week, or at the end of the sprint. The author determines which documents are impacted (as one person may author several documents) and then updates it. Some authors can write their documents from scratch and just need an SME/peer to do a tech edit. I've known more than one application architect to do this. I also make sure everyone has access to the same RMS the developers are using.

Lastly, I use the DARR chart, the Optimal BRC, and the Doc Prep Checklist on almost every project, either in part or entirely. The DARR and the Optimal BRC get modified almost every project, but the Doc Prep Checklist decisions stay pretty much the same. The others I use occasionally. I always data-slim the doc pack, even if I have to do it myself.

Gorillas Do Not Wait

Gorillas know the key to the quality and accuracy of Agile project documents is not waiting to build them until close to delivery. I know that's not what you Agile gurus promote because of stability of features and cost, but your "just barely good enough" documents will become "just barely shitty enough" if you wait too long. But hey, if you don't care, I don't. Push them rags through that meat grinder and get them to your customer, Pal; I'm not putting my name on that shit though. It's all you.

Seriously, building documents close to the delivery date will damage the quality or the documents simply won't get completed. As I have said before, documents are not a priority, they are a requirement. The priority is the application. But waiting that late will make them *become* a priority, whether the team likes it or not, and everybody assigned to produce these documents will suffer.

On most projects, each person, whether they are a developer, a business analyst, an application architect, or whatever, will be required to author all (or at least some part) of a document. The technical writer will be assisting. If the document package consists of fifty or so documents and everybody waits until delivery time, it will be difficult for the tech writer to be able to write his/her documents *and* do a copy edit on everyone else's.

The review cycle will be needlessly clogged up too. So, gorillas don't wait.

Lacking confidence in any or all of the following does not provide a good reason to wait until the end of cycle to produce the documents:
- The requirements
- Requirement stability
- The development team
- The change management process

In my humble opinion, the only reasons to wait to the end of cycle or close to delivery to produce the documents are either because the business owner can't make up his/her mind or because the business's needs are simply changing. If that's the case, it may be best to postpone the entire project until *both* stabilize. Otherwise the "feature creep monster" will be dragging the project backwards and forwards through requirement hell. The good news is, a smart gorilla trumps the feature creep monster every time.

I have my authors use multi-channel authoring software that makes changes easy, as well as a process that does too.

Additionally, requirements-gathering should be precise with an analyst that has a good track record of getting the requirements right. I know many businesses have an "I'll know it when I see it" attitude, and I get that. Just make sure they "see it" early.

Review Cycles

See the "BRC" tabs on the spreadsheets.

Gorillas use two types of review cycles: mini and final. Mini review cycles can be run in between delivery dates and milestones. They make things much easier when it comes to delivery and the final review. By that time, most issues with the doc package are resolved. Anytime I've conducted just a final review at the end, I've had issues that consumed way too much time from the team. Sometimes I had to leave stuff out just to make the deadline. It's not good.

Starting the final review cycle two weeks before delivery time is optimal; one week is minimal — especially with thirty-day sprints. It depends of the amount of documentation deliverables and available assets. This allows time for edits, comment incorporation, arguments about comments, fact-checking, validation, and so forth. I have had final review cycles three days before delivery, but we had plenty of assets and few documents with small pagination. I wouldn't recommend it though. Talk about a Three Stooges fire drill. . . .

If there is a five-to-fifteen-day user acceptance testing (UAT) period after the last sprint, the documents should be completed and ready to be delivered to the new owner. If there are changes to be made from the results of UAT, then I incorporate them and edit them in place. If they require a tech edit, I request for the SME or author to do it and have them email me when they are finished.

Meetings

Gorillas don't like lots of meetings, because they chew up time and money.

Have a one-hour hard stop for each of the following:

- Lean writing
- Determining the doc pack
- Assigning authors and other roles (People Tracker)
- Complete the Doc Prep Checklist
- Data-slimming

A gorilla—preferably a PM—should run these meetings and keep them on track. No bullshit sessions about weekend drunkery, football games, or the latest handbags on whatever shopping channel. Get in, get it done, and get out; that's the deal. Unless, of course, the meetings are at the pub.

In some circles, the doc pack and assigned roles are pre-determined or the PM does this alone. If that's the case, the PM brings those assignments to the Doc Prep meeting and the team goes from there. After the docs are framed and before the build, the data slim is conducted. After that, it's emails, phone calls, and cube visits. Cut the document meetings to *zero*, unless absolutely necessary. They quickly become counterproductive.

Updates

As I have outlined in the definition section, an update can be one of four things:

- Changing to existing material (e.g., "four" servers being used changed to "five")
- Deleting existing material

- Adding new material (text from single words up to entire topics)
    o If you are adding whole sections, the document is still being built.
    o Adding new material also includes adding graphics.
- Changing structure or the sequence of modules (no text or graphics deleted or modified)

I use the term "update" in the spreadsheets to denote one of these four changes. Making an update to a document may or may not require a trip through the review process. A build always does. If I deliver a partially-built user guide, for example — say sections 1-5 out of 10 sections completed and versioned 1.0 — then it is still being built. So, in the next iteration — in which sections 6-10 would be populated and versioned 1.1 or 2.0 — the document goes through the same build process that it did with sections 1-5. I do not consider sections 6-10 as updates.

Update Management

Each author is responsible for the updates to his/her document. At the very least, if a certain section is impacted by a change in requirements, the contributor of that section is responsible. An update path can be anything, so long as it is accepted and efficient.

For example, an author is perusing the RMS and sees that a feature has been modified. He/she then implements that modification in his/her corresponding document or is set up to receive alerts to changes in requirements within the RMS (not all systems do this).

Or, for another example, I have had developers/architects come directly to my desk and say, "Hey, I changed this," and we would go through my assigned document (usually the user guide) and make the change.

There is no perfect system I could outline for each and every project for each and every organization. I expect change and plan for it. When it happens, I think of ways to streamline it and make it better and faster. I use the gorilla rules for updates to help me.

For updates, gorillas do the following:

- Outline a specific process for each document (can be done as part of the Doc Prep Checklist, but may change over time)
- Use Track Changes or some commenting function
    - Sometimes organizations use spreadsheets to track comments and their adjudication process. I hate this method because it adds more documents. But if the org has constant back-and-forth battles over comments, it might be worth using spreadsheets to avoid millions of Track Changes bubbles all over your document.
- Use an effective review cycle if and when necessary
- Use the spreadsheets that come with this book
- Use authoring software that makes changes easy (drag-and-drop TOC modules are nice)
- Use reference materials and SMEs as outlined in the Doc Prep Checklist
- Peruse the RMS
- Are proactive
    - When changes are made, the people that made them are not always in a hurry to inform the impacted personnel.

I also try to reuse material as much as I can. That way, if I have a graphic or topic used in one document but referenced by three others, and I have to update that topic or graphic, I only have to do it in one place.

Additionally, I try to get a feel for the amount of changes we might get during a sprint by analyzing the development group. If the development group members are experienced, they will most likely get the requirements right the first time and once these requirements are coded, they will stay. So the authors and tech writers will be making very few changes to existing data in the docs. If the development group is inexperienced, its members have a tendency to change/fix the features and or code. So things like the SDD, ADD, and user guide may change frequently. But it's Agile, or a modified version of it, so that's the deal.

The Online Document Package

Combine All the Word Documents—If Possible

I have a multichannel authoring system, so I always see if producing an online doc pack is possible. I import all my Word documents and give them their own folder. This way, the doc pack is one file. I xref and hyperlink sections and graphics between documents, when possible, further reducing redundancy and interconnecting relevant data. I work with the PM and other authors to help identify sections with Track Changes bubbles that should be cross-referenced with other sections in different documents. It's a way of interconnecting data, but only if it's deemed necessary.

The one drawback is that all the documents are one file/project. Team members need to access it, and that becomes problematic in a CMS because only one person at a time can check it out for editing. However, I usually wait until the document is completed, then import the word files into my authoring system and publish one file. Once it's finished, it's an excellent product.

Example of an Online Doc Package

HTML Help format (cropped of course):

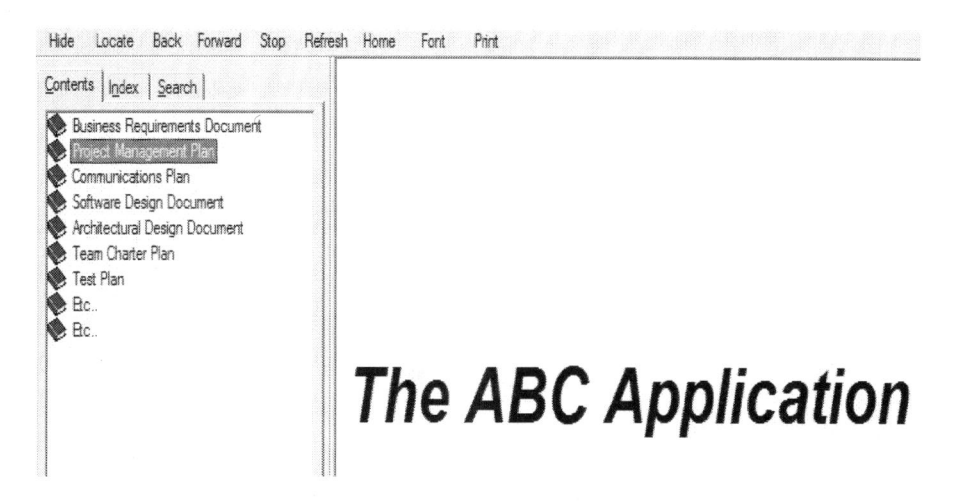

```
Hide  Locate  Back  Forward  Stop  Refresh  Home  Font  Print

Contents | Index | Search
   Business Requirements Document
   Project Management Plan
   Communications Plan
   Software Design Document
   Architectural Design Document
   Team Charter Plan
   Test Plan
   Etc..
   Etc..
```

The ABC Application

Combine the User Guide and Training Materials

I also like to interconnect the user guide and training materials. I don't like mixing different types of topics unless absolutely necessary. One of the biggest problems with user guides is that authors try to merge concept and task topics in one user guide.

The training materials are specifically written to educate, while the user guide's main goal is to guide a user through a task. The training guide is concept-oriented and the user guide is task-oriented, but the two can be directly related.

For example, if a user wants to complete a task, he/she navigates to the task in the user guide. If the user needs it explained further, he/she simply clicks one of the related links at the bottom or top of the task. The training guide then opens in a different window to the section that explains in greater depth what the system does for that particular task. The military calls it the theory of ops section, but they also use it to train people as well.

I find it incredibly beneficial to use xrefs or to cross-reference related topics between the training guide / theory of ops and the user guide. Additionally, the trainers can use a combined package for the same purpose. The training guide has links to its corresponding tasks in the user guide and vice versa, so it's a two-way street.

Example of a User Guide / Training Material Package

HTML Help format:

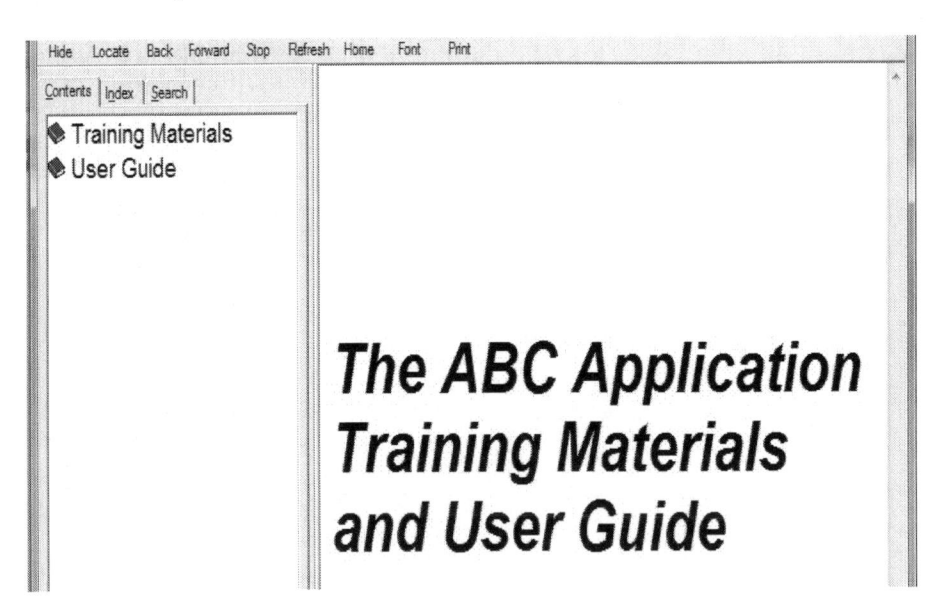

![Screenshot of HTML Help window showing Contents pane with "Training Materials" and "User Guide" entries, and main pane displaying "The ABC Application Training Materials and User Guide"]

Below is an example of linking the training materials with the user guide. In this fictitious example, I hyperlinked both the bulleted items at the top of the page and the tasks at the bottom to their associated tasks in the user guide. Normally, I would do one or the other, though, not both.

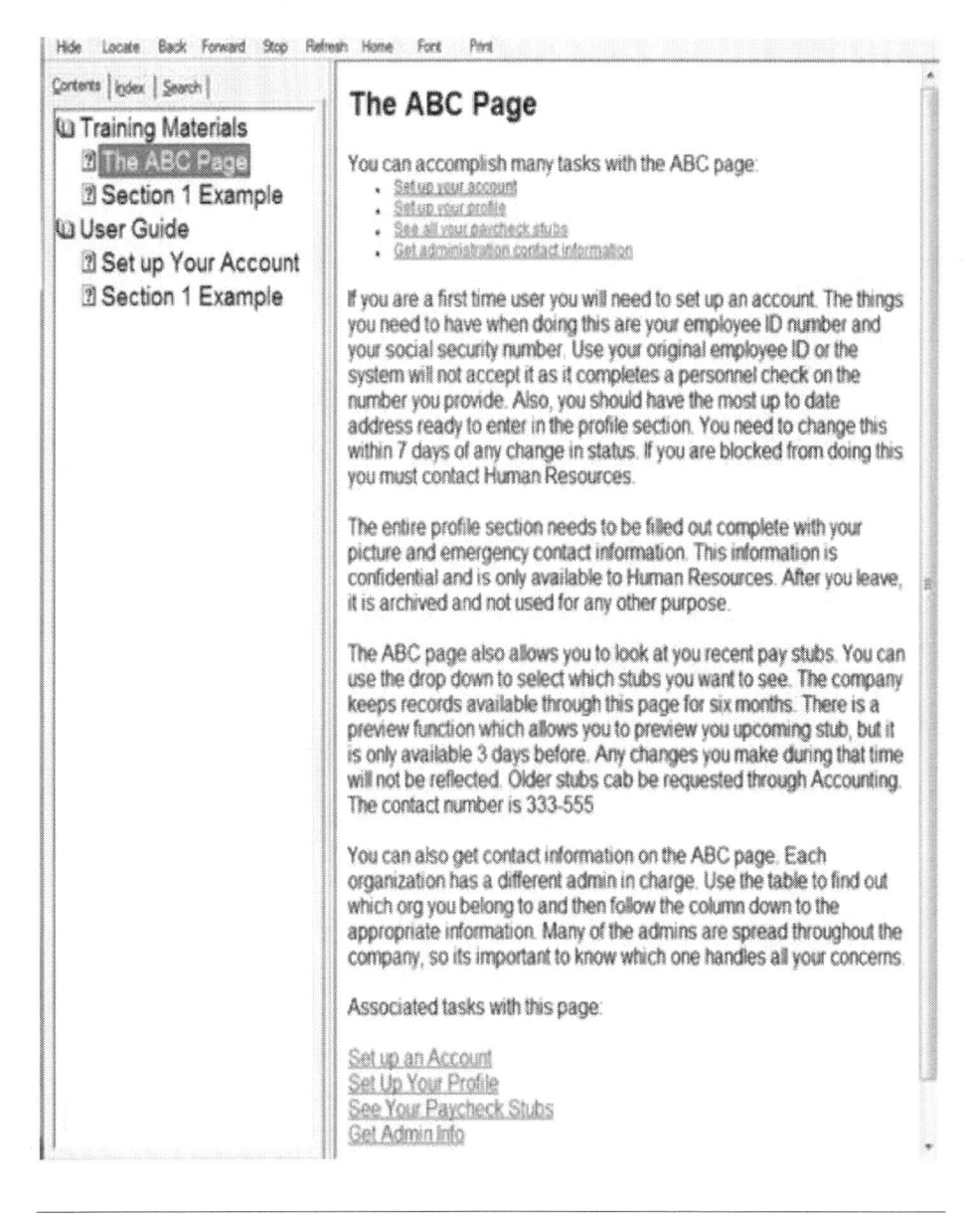

```
Hide  Locate  Back  Forward  Stop  Refresh  Home  Font  Print
Contents | Index | Search |
```

Training Materials 　The ABC Page 　Section 1 Example User Guide 　Set up Your Account 　Section 1 Example	**The ABC Page** You can accomplish many tasks with the ABC page: • Set up your account • Set up your profile • See all your paycheck stubs • Get administration contact information If you are a first time user you will need to set up an account. The things you need to have when doing this are your employee ID number and your social security number. Use your original employee ID or the system will not accept it as it completes a personnel check on the number you provide. Also, you should have the most up to date address ready to enter in the profile section. You need to change this within 7 days of any change in status. If you are blocked from doing this you must contact Human Resources. The entire profile section needs to be filled out complete with your picture and emergency contact information. This information is confidential and is only available to Human Resources. After you leave, it is archived and not used for any other purpose. The ABC page also allows you to look at you recent pay stubs. You can use the drop down to select which stubs you want to see. The company keeps records available through this page for six months. There is a preview function which allows you to preview your upcoming stub, but it is only available 3 days before. Any changes you make during that time will not be reflected. Older stubs cab be requested through Accounting. The contact number is 333-555 You can also get contact information on the ABC page. Each organization has a different admin in charge. Use the table to find out which org you belong to and then follow the column down to the appropriate information. Many of the admins are spread throughout the company, so its important to know which one handles all your concerns. Associated tasks with this page: Set up an Account Set Up Your Profile See Your Paycheck Stubs Get Admin Info

In the example below, I used an xref—which grabs the title of what you link it to—from the task to the training materials. This way, if the user needs to find out more about the page or the task, all he/she needs to do is click the link. I usually have the link open in another window so the user can look at both.

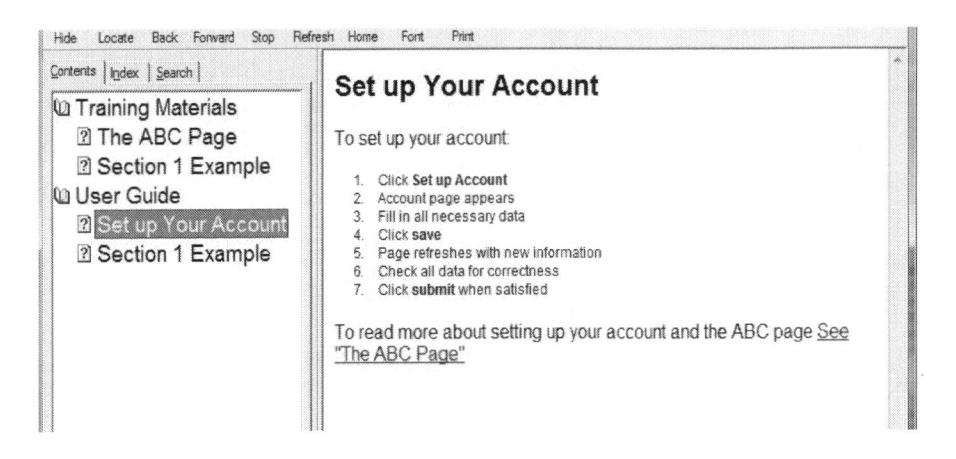

Gorilla Rules for Phasing Documents

- Focus on the initiate/inception documents in the initiate/inception phase.
- Create the rest of the project documents in the plan phase.
- Designate an open/close document time.
- Build the documents as soon as there is data, but with a predesigned process.
- Try to get technical edits by SMEs/peers done throughout the development cycle.
- Start the final review cycle one to two weeks before the end of the delivery date.

Focus on the Initiate/Inception Documents in the Initiate/Inception Phase

This allows for the best possible documents (phase-wise) to get the project off the ground. Create, build, complete, and sign-off whichever documents are required to start the project, such as the Project Management Plan, CONOPS, BRD, Team Plan, Schedule Tracking documents, Legal Authority, Reason-to-Be, Gimme Money, and Green-Light docs. As I have learned from past projects, even these supposedly "finished" documents have been updated while the project was in development, so any document can be updated at any time, depending on the organization. I just have a change process in place. Focus on the documents that get the project off the ground first, then focus on the others.

Additionally, the review process may be very short — if it happens at all — with some of these documents, as some of them may be only one page long or may simply be a checklist. If that's the case, the review cycle may consist of only one author, an editor (either technical, business, or legal), and a sign-off (Tower Lead, Director, Program Manager, etc.).

Create the Rest of the Project Documents in the Plan Phase

Whatever document is not considered a green-light document needs to be created in the plan phase. This means having templates (or at least some sort of semi-framed documents) complete with proper titles *and* having them located in the proper directory ready to accept data. Completing the Doc Prep Checklist is optimal. That way, there will be no scrambling for templates or design meetings when it's build time.

Designate an Open/Close Document Time

I control when the documents are available for adding data. I send an email with a link to all authors when documents are opened. Additionally, I close the documents just prior to running the final review cycle. I try to do it for a mini review as well. For an effective and efficient cycle, a "pens down" date is necessary. Adding data while final review is going on is confusing, hard to track, and quite frankly stupid. It's like bailing water out of your fishing boat while your buddy is scooping water from the lake and dumping it in and then saying "Dude, why the fuck are we sinking?" When the documents are in a CMS, access control is easy. But I lock the docs before the final review.

Build the Documents as Soon as There Is Data, but with a Predesigned Process

Workload, asset restrictions, and data limitations may not allow for all documents to be built in the plan phase, for example, but I drop them in the workflow and open them as soon as possible. Usually, most project documents (SDD, ADD, user guides, etc.,) are opened to build when the develop/execute phase starts. Some documents are opened during the last sprint, some during the test phase. I determine what's best for the docs by working with the authors and the PM.

For example, say an author peruses RMS for new updates daily or weekly; a developer/tester gives the author completed features in scratch documents to be put in the user guide every Friday *or* when there is determined to be enough data that hopefully will not change. *Or*, the author is extrapolating acceptance criteria and test cases to build the user guide.

If the data comes in at different times, then so be it. The authors and teams have to deal with it. The same goes for features that are either deleted or changed.

Try to Get Technical Edits by SMEs/Peers Done throughout the Development Cycle

It is far easier to complete simple copy editing close to delivery than it is to complete technical editing. Especially if you have to do both for all the material. Technical editing is much slower and thought-intensive. But, for sure, I start that final review cycle two weeks prior to delivery. The team needs the time.

Start the Final Review Cycle One to Two Weeks before the End of the Delivery Date

This, of course, will depend on assets, their allotted time, sprint/cycle duration, and workload. The closer to the delivery date the review is started, the shittier the quality. The further out the final review cycle is started from the delivery date, the more time there will be to incorporate comments and ensure a quality document. The same goes for testing. There will most likely be additional changes from the testers/team; I make sure the review cycle is set up for it.

With Short Iteration Cycles, Sometimes You Can Document after Complete

Thirty-day sprints almost necessitate that the docs be built and updated as soon as there is data. However, with two-week sprints, it's possible to document what was built in a given sprint, in the following sprint. If this happens, though, the team will be two weeks behind. If the project calls for a delivery at the end of sprint 3, for example, obviously, they will be late or have to hustle to make delivery.

If, however, a UAT period exists — or perhaps a hardening sprint, as it does with mixed models of Agile — then perhaps it's possible.

I don't like this method, because the team purposely puts itself behind the eight ball. With one- and two-week sprints, it may be inevitable, but enough shit is going to happen during the project that puts the team behind anyway, so why add to it?

A Word on Hardening Sprints

Not a big fan. It helps the authors and technical writers somewhat, because they can complete final tasks before delivery. Waterfall folks like it. But, hardening sprints screw up the "Definition of Done." It lets the team build up technical debt (code cleanup and other things) that is left to clear during this iteration, so delivery has to wait until the end of this sprint anyway. Not good practice. Doesn't jive with Scrum either. In my humble opinion.

Phased Documentation

See the DARR chart, BRC, Milestone, and Doc Tracker tabs in the spreadsheets

Gorillas know there is a time and place for every document. It needs to be planned. With different Agile projects I've worked on, I usually hear the phrase, "We'll create it when we need it." This seems to be standard Agile procedure, and I've heard more than one PM say it. Unfortunately, many times their "need" occurs at the last minute. Well, no shit if it's required and not created. At that point it's usually slapped together with no QA and very little thought behind it, because he/she doesn't care. The design usually sucks and no one uses it.

The spreadsheets included with this book should give you an idea how I "phase" documentation. Meaning, which documents I create, build, and complete, and when. Throughout the last eight years, I have seen twenty different variations of the Agile/Waterfall/Iterative/etc., process. Some organizations mix them, some are true, and some make up their own. So these models are not all-inclusive. One PM I knew put it best: "Once you start mixing models, then there is no model." The PM should know what his/her organization's phase diagram looks like. If not, he/she should build a visual representation of it then plug in the right documents and the best times to create, build, and complete them.

I like to use the spreadsheets included with this book at the first planning meeting for the documents; sometimes I use a PowerPoint. I have found that having some sort of visual aid really helps people understand the process.

Maintaining Documents after Deployment or Final Delivery

Once the application either goes into deployment or gets delivered, the documents are no longer the team's headache, unless there are multiple deliveries. This section will address some of those concerns but will not go into great depth, because it's out of the scope of this book. And really, I don't feel like writing about it.

If a project requires several versions of the same application or delivery dates/milestones with increased functionality with each iteration, the process stays the same with the documents. The final review cycle is run one to two weeks prior to delivery, etc. It's pretty much the same as the application.

Upon final delivery, the document package goes to its new owner who will need to determine the document update process, if it hasn't been determined already. If the application and its documents were built *by and for* the same company, the technical writers may be tasked with doing updates at least for a time. This happens from time to time. Throw the docs over the wall to ops and they don't have the resources. Ah well, guess we can't kick the kids out of the house yet. . . .

Usually, the new owner wants to do the updates, leaving the tech writers out of it, but they need the capability. Obviously, the new owner's authoring software should be the same type and version that the documents were created with. This should have been determined during the build process. The new owner should at least have the ability to import and export one compatible format.

If the app was built for and by the same company, but it's going to a different unit/division/site/plant, etc., then the editing software should be on the IT list and should be easily downloadable by the new owner if he/she doesn't have it already.

Most of the document package stays as-is with the exception of a few that will need updates, such as the SDD, ADD, perhaps training materials, and of course, the user guide. If one of my projects doesn't require a user guide, yay for me—less I have to do. User guides have a few special considerations, because they usually get updated the most and they may be in an online format with CSH.

Special Considerations for the User Guide

Most of the doc pack will not need to be accessed by users in the field. The user guide, however, is arguably the most accessed document that the team creates. It also should be a living document. If the application is deployed to one site and the help is in one directory on the company server, access should be easy on the company's intranet. But when the application is deployed to several sites, there is no intranet, several networks exist, and/or access to the Internet is limited or non-existent, I feel there are some major concerns:

- Does the new owner (site, ops, client, whoever) have the correct application to update the help?
- Will the help be embedded with the application or in one place on a server or CMS somewhere? (Crucial to know if the application goes out to multiple sites.)

Will the Help Be Embedded with the Application or in One Place?

One-Place Pros

- Updates are done at a central location and all applications linked to it will have the updated information simultaneously.
- Only one person/entity needs to do it, but can receive updates from other sites to incorporate into new version of help.

- If all sites have Internet access, help should be readily available.
- If multiple sites have input for updates, they send them to one place/person. (This will ensure uniformity and QA.)

One-Place Cons

- If there is no Internet access, help may not be readily available.
- If multiple sites have input for updates, they send them to one place/person. (This could be problematic depending on the entities involved.)
- If the sites are on separate networks, all sites may not have access to the help, as some may be down while others are up.
- The network that the help system is on can be down and kill all sites' help, unless there is a help system backup at each site.
- Your networks may not support the bandwidth necessary for fast and efficient help (this may be problematic if there are many users at multiple sites accessing the data).

Embedded-Help Pros

- Updates would be done at the site, perhaps making them faster and easier.
- Updates to the help can be site-specific (the updates may not apply to other sites).
- The site will not have to submit changes to the central location and wait for changes to appear.
- If your application is up, your help should be up too. If it's down, there won't be any need to worry about the help.

Embedded-Help Cons

- Sites will need to submit changes to the central location and perhaps wait on updates.
- Updates from one site may not be necessary at other sites.
- Updates from one site may not be uniform with other sites, and after a time the help may look completely different.
- Updates found necessary at one site may not be readily disseminated.

These considerations are not always the project team's headache. They may be left to the new owner who may in turn have to deal with a new application that needs to be distributed company-wide with all of its documents. But these questions need to be answered, and I make sure they are in step 5.0 of the Doc Prep Checklist.

Context-Sensitive Help (CSH)

If the client requires a CSH user guide, the project team needs to work with the development team and business owner in the planning stage. (It was also a consideration in step 5 of the document build process). The development team will say what they need insofar as CSH is concerned. It's usually files in the form of alias and header files. Basically, the technical writer provides the linking mechanism with the authoring software and the development team links to it.

The business owner should have an idea as to what topics/sections/areas they need to be context sensitive. Additionally, only certain formats support CSH.

Lastly, it also affects the bottom line, as it is a bit more intensive for the technical writers and developers. So doing some research before engaging in CSH is crucial. Otherwise, you may be wandering into a labyrinth of bullshit the likes of which Dante could not have imagined. And I like Dante.

There are entire books and sections of books dedicated to CSH; this isn't one of them. So if you want to learn about it, start googling.

Planning and Estimating Tools: User Stories to Man-Hours

Gorillas like to plan, as I said before, so planning and estimation metrics to assist in calculating create, build, review, and complete times in man-hours are great tools. It's fairly easy to estimate document creation times from scratch. Many times, however, estimating how much effort in man-hours it will take to complete a document based on the software requirements (user stories) is difficult. It's even more difficult to estimate a document's man-hours with multiple contributors. However, I have been fairly successful at estimating the effort in man-hours based on the user stories for a number of projects using past projects as a reference.

To obtain these estimations, I had to add up all the effort in direct man-hours (meaning those from the author and technical writer) and indirect man-hours (such as those from the SME's technical edits and sign-off personnel). Contributory authors' actual man-hours were a challenge to nail down as well, due to the partial nature of their involvement. I had to base my metrics on their estimations. For some reason, the author's actual man-hours per project were much easier. Authors had a clearer picture of how much time they spent creating a document. Technical writers were the easiest, as they simply bill their man-hours to each project. Even the technical writers' times got tricky, though, when they were tasked with multiple documents. Unfortunately, though, I couldn't get metrics on every type of document.

User Guide

The following tables represent an average for the metrics I gathered for user guides:

1 story=9 steps=2 pages=10 total man-hours (SRC) 14 (LRC)

User Stories	Steps	Pages	Total Man-Hours (SRC)	Total Man-Hours (LRC)
1	9	2	10	14

And per page:

Pages	Build man hours	Tech Review man-hours	Comment Adjudication man-hours	Copy Edit man hours	Output Edit man-hours	Total SRC man hours	Total LRC man hours
1	2	1	1	0.5	0.5	5	7

These tables assume a 70/30 split on text to graphics. SRC is short review cycle, LRC is long review cycle. There is also a 10% variable on all numbers except Stories and Pages. Comment Adjudication includes "clarification" times between the author and the comment owner, but can be 0.5 hours. LRC can include validation. User stories averaged 3 points.

Here is one example of a user guide build formula I calculated after completion:

Assets	Stories	Topics	Pages	Total Man-Hours
2	50	55	98	650

The above metric for a user guide was above the average. It received a minimal review cycle and all information was extrapolated from a BRD, acceptance criteria, and the test environment. Compiling the data took a bit longer, because the information was difficult to extrapolate. Most steps were also validated, so this metric included part of a long review cycle.

The document grade was about a B-. Features were medium, writing was decent, and complexity was medium. Some screenshots (75/25 text-to-graphics split) and output to PDF from authoring software.

Not every user story was a user guide entry. Functional requirements had to be differentiated from non-functional and the necessity of any particular story for the user guide had to be determined. In this case there were 50 stories, which turned into 55 topics. Non-functional requirements (speeds and feeds) are rarely a part of a user guide unless they are necessary to an administrator or network-type person. However, I have put such non-functional requirements in installation guides and training materials on other projects.

Installation Guide

Another project:

Authors	Tech Editors	Tech Writer	Pages	Total Man-Hours
5	3	1	630	3100

630 pages, 3 authors, 2 SMEs doing rewrites, and 3 SMEs doing tech edits, and me.

Actuals (figures are rounded):

- For the 3 authors and 2 SMEs: 2,150 man-hours total
- For the tech edit SMEs: 400 man-hours total
- My contribution: 550 hours total
- Total: 3,100 man-hours in effort to produce this 630 page Installation Guide

Minimal BRC on this one. I did all the editing. No sign-off. Low complexity. No features except text and graphics. Structure changed no less than twenty times. Data changes were weekly. Authors wrote the document from scratch — no stories. Text-to-graphics split was about 60/40; a heavy document. Final product was about a C+.

These are the metrics built from averages that worked for me on different projects. Metrics on any given project vary and everybody's metrics are different. That's why I like producing samples.

Factors That Determine Create-Build-Complete (CBC) Times

There are a number of factors that determine create, build, and complete man-hours, but the main ones are:

- The number of user stories.
- Complexity.
- The number of document features (more features require more time).
- The graphic/text percentage split (60/40, 70/30, etc.). More graphics require more time and increase the file size of the document. (Search for .PNG, .JPEG, .SVG, .BMP, and other formats on Google for pros and cons of each.)
- Desired quality level. (A, B, C, D, as in grade; lower is faster).
- The speed and efficiency of personnel and data flow.
- The chosen build and review process (shorter is faster, longer is usually slower).
- The stability of application features *can* affect CBC times.

Test Runs for CBC Times

Conducting a test BRC to estimate accurate CBC times is optimal. It doesn't take much effort. If done in the planning stage, test BRC runs give the PM an accurate account of actual times to build and review certain documents that he/she can use when the project starts.

I run them whenever possible but only on the most important document(s), like the user guide. It doesn't take that much effort up front, but it can save you lots of trouble on the back end.

To complete a test, I just pick a user story or two from the RMS that has good stability, run a BRC, and track the man-hours of effort from the author, contributors, SMEs, editors, technical writers, and sign off personnel.

Document Quality Level

The quality level I shoot for is C+. I know for all you writers and editors this is like blasphemy, but that's what it is. If you're like me, you're tasked out to several projects, swimming in documents, low on assets, and constantly on a time crunch. So I have neither the time nor the inclination to produce a perfect A+ document. I keep them as simple and utilitarian as I can. If I can skip the pretty bullshit I will, especially if it needs to get out the door most riki tik.

Having C+-grade informational documents is where bang meets buck. Cost benefits analysis usually reveals that A+ documentation is not cost effective. And while D- documentation may be the cheapest, it's just shit the team rolled out knowing nobody would use. If that's the case, I wouldn't even bother. I'd save myself even more time and money by not doing them, *or* optimize/streamline them out in the initiate/plan phase or the doc pack meeting.

Most organizations have standards, but few actually enforce them. Some even have grading matrices and evaluation checklists to sample documentation. These, in my experience, were used for contractors as a yardstick, and the internal ones I saw were rarely used. Nobody wants to get called on their own garbage. Good and bad may be subjective, but when it comes down to it, those are the only terms people use. So why not meet them in the middle? Fortunately, that's where the value is.

Most technical writers are not concerned with money and time like PMs are. They care about birthing the best possible product and being proud authors. That's cool; that's what they're taught. If time and money are abundant, there's no problem; let them run.

I don't have that luxury, so I shoot for decent documents completed with the fewest amount of assets in the least amount of time. I'm given deadlines that stick and I don't take my work home. Quality is on a sliding scale and I want mine to read C+. I'm not trying to build a Mercedes with Hyundai money. There is a balance between quality and time that exists, and every PM has to find it.

Truth be told, my C+ is probably a B+ by most people's standards. I'm just critical of my own work.

Oh, and "just barely good enough"? If I had to grade all the "JBGE" documents I've seen in the last eight years, I'd give them a D-. Some worse, very few better, but none ever exceeded a C.

Characteristics of a C+ Document

- **CRUCIAL:** It is written so that the user only has to read the text once to understand, not multiple times.
- It uses pithy, terse writing—not eloquent prose; may seem choppy to the literary sect.
- It is halfway between high school writing and bullets.
- It uses subject-verb-object sentence structure.
- It uses a minimalistic writing style (see "Tactical Minimalism").
- It uses a minimal amount of complex words.
- It scores between a ninth- and twelfth-grade level on the reading indexes.
- It uses modular/topic-based construction.
- It has only the features deemed necessary to be efficient and utilitarian.
- It has a 70/30 text-to-graphics split, or close to it.
- It doesn't have any redundancies with itself or other documents.
- A sample has been approved by a user or someone on the business side.

Writing: Conventions, Philosophy, and Style

This book is not a guide on how to write. That's why this stuff is at the end. It's the least important part of the book. There are a thousand books on the subject already, so why write one more? However, there are a few things that I consider worth mentioning.

This collection of writing philosophies and conventions includes some of what I feel relevant to writers and authors within the IT field. This list is by no means conclusive, and I would encourage authors, whoever they may be, to research these terms and other good writing practices.

Philosophies

Client-Centred Writing: Audience Analyses

Gorillas like to know the audience to some degree — at the very least, their capabilities in understanding a particular section. Are they a manager type, administrator, line user, business person, or a tech head?
Once the target audience/reader is identified, the language is tailored to what would most connect with them. The writing must speak the reader's language and use a voice that resonates with them.

Additionally, the material must be organized in terms of what matters to the reader.

Google: Personas, Writing genres

Tactical Minimalism

Gorillas don't like to write too much. They say what they need to say using the fewest amount of words, and the reader understands what is communicated in one pass. Some authors, however, suffer from Baron von Wordhausen syndrome, and the reader has to go back over the text and read it a few times. To avoid this syndrome, I:

- **Read my text out loud**. Or, I use that text-reading software. This is crucial. I can hear my clunkers. If I get tripped up speaking it, the audience will get tripped up reading it.
- **Pare it down**. No wordy stuff. I don't need all those adjectives some people have in their sentences. My writing is halfway between high school writing and bullets.
- **Don't use fancy stuff**. I leave all those big words in the dictionary. It doesn't make me sound any smarter by using them, so I don't try to be a pretentious prick. Ornate words? If I have to crank up the dictionary function on Word to pick a word, I don't use it.
- **Communicate thoughts and ideas.** The best way to do this is by being simple. The delivery method for my content is a mode that the audience understands. If I want to hear myself talk I do it in the shower, but I don't kill my audience with textual genocide.

Examples of Applied Tactical Minimalism:

Original Text:

System Architecture

Ozone WebSys is the application server that is used by ABC applications. Current WebSys domain configuration is going to be changed as result of the XYZ application technology, which is being refreshed and is included in the XYZ Simon Says Program. The XYZ netting application has to change from a D-based application with a T-based on UNITS curses archive into a DEUCE application with a Web Interface. As other DEUCE-based applications, like EFS, it has to use the correct features of the Ozone WebSys server for caching and pooling. XYZ will be using enterprise-managed transactions. These transactions will be managed by the Ozone WebSys Application Server.
Previous XYZ as a DEF module does not use transaction management because its mechanism is chiefly asynchronous. DEF applications use cross-process communication protocols to asynchronously transfer data from one service to another. New XYZ is a critical application, and, because of that, the WebSys server design needs to guarantee as many resources as so it will not create performance issues.
Below, you can see the proposed WebSys configuration for the XYZ Simon Says Program.

Minimalized Reboot:

System Architecture

Ozone WebSys is the application server used by ABC applications.

Proposed Domain Configuration

Current WebSys domain configuration will be changed because of the XYZ application technology refreshment included in the XYZ Simon Says Program. XYZ netting application will change from a D-based application with a T-based on UNITS curses archive into a DEUCE application with a Web Interface. New XYZ is critical and will use enterprise-managed transactions. So, to prevent performance issues, the WebSys server design must provide as many resources as possible.

The graphic below illustrates the proposed WebSys configuration for the XYZ Simon Says Program.

Here, 189 words were cut to 101 *and* the information is in the right place. That's nearly a 47% reduction. Plus, all but one sentence was under the wrong header in the original text. And this is just the writing. Strictly though, the first sentence under "System Architecture" is the only one that belongs, because the other paragraph is speculative stuff. This example attempts to explain the "to-be design" and why. So there was some latitude. Another (from this book):

We will use five **SupaFast servers** *[new and now-known info] for the new data center. These* **Supafast servers** *[known info] have* **a bandwidth of 123 and a speed of 456** *[new info]. With a speed of 456, they are extremely efficient and able to accommodate 200 users. Your company needs the ability for 200 users to be logged on simultaneously to handle the massive amount of data input for the ABC task.*

Minimalized reboot:

The data center uses five (5) Supafast servers with a bandwidth of 123, a speed of 456, and can accommodate 200 users simultaneously.

OR: The data center uses:
5 Supafast servers with:
- 123 bandwidth
- 456 speed
- 200 user-at-once capability

The last "Your company . . ." sentence is unnecessary sales stuff. Here, 64 words were cut to 17. Even though the corrected text is an informational solution to a persuasion paragraph, this is what I find exists in informational documents—and it doesn't need to.

To Apply Tactical Minimalism

- Don't use history lessons ("Previous systems did this . . ." "Ozone systems tended to . . .")
    - Good for persuasive documents
- Don't use comparisons ("The old system did this . . ." "Commercial systems do this . . .")
    - Good for persuasive documents
- Clean out the adjectives. Most people use too many.
- Use bullets where possible, but don't overuse.
- Look for ways to shorten sentences.
- Scan topics for useless sentences.
    - Data-slimming should have removed useless or redundant modules.
- Write only what the system does.
- Don't use big words unless they are necessary technical terms.
- Use the smallest, tightest, most muscular words in your vocabulary.
- Don't use any qualifier sentences or paragraphs ("We did this because . . ." "This is because . . ." "Only if . . ." "Sometimes when . . ." "Users will need this because . . ."). If it's a green-light document and you're trying to sell your project, these phrases

are fine. But in that case, it is a persuasion document and you have more latitude.

Minimalism — it will save you money. I can't say that enough.

Minimalism — it will save you money. Okay, okay. . . . Jeez.

And if you don't believe me, read this quote from Papa Gorilla:

"Poor Faulkner. Does he really think big emotions come from big words? He thinks I don't know the ten-dollar words. I know them all right. But there are older and simpler and better words, and those are the ones I use."

Ernest Hemingway

Or from a great inventor:

"Simplicity is the ultimate form of sophistication."

Leonardo da Vinci

Or from someone you've never heard of until today:

"Never confuse complexity with intelligence; the use of simplicity makes scholars of us all."

"Simplicity is the sincerest form of intelligence."

"You need examples? The atom, in all its simplistic beauty, is the building block of the universe, while the LA freeway system, the Metrorail fair tables, and the congressional bill review process are the bane of it."

Me

Techniques

The Known-New Contract

I learned this in school, so this is what I can remember:

"The 'known-new contract' is a linguistic concept that describes how writers maintain cohesion of thought for their readers between sentences and paragraphs."

Google the term for a further explanation, but this technique involves using the information in a previous sentence's predicate as the subject of the sentence that follows it. The known-new concept is best used in an explanation or in a conceptual paragraph.

The following example is not minimalized writing but is something you might find in a proposal where expository writing gets more latitude:

We will use five **SupaFast servers** *[new and now-known info] for the new data center. These* **Supafast servers** *[known info] have a* **bandwidth of 123 and a speed of 456** *[new info]. With a speed of 456, they are extremely efficient and able to accommodate 200 users. Your company needs the ability for 200 users to be logged on simultaneously to handle the massive amount of data input for the ABC task.*

Once the ABC task has been started . . .

You get the idea. Generally, if you use the predicate of a sentence — which is known — as the subject of the following sentence, the predicate of that sentence can contain new information.

This method is extremely well-suited for technical people to explain detailed and complex technical information to non-techies. It's linear, easy to follow, and there is a clear beginning and end.

Long Sentences Punctuated by a Short Declarative Sentence

Example:

For ten years your data center has used the inefficient and outdated ABC model server that has been creating problems for your company. **Our team uses a different server.** *We use the DEF model, which has more capability, is faster, and can fill all your specific needs as it has ours.*

The short sentence is like a dramatic pause. It makes the reader stop, put an end to the preceding information, and prepare for the next sentence, which — due to the pause — will set the stage for the right solution. A short, strong statement is especially good for transitioning from something that is bad to something that is good — all within the confines of a paragraph.

Use this convention sparingly and when you want to make an important point.

Connect Paragraphs to Ease the Transition for the Reader

Use the bottom of a paragraph to intro its succeeding paragraph.

Example:

For ten years your data center has used the inefficient and outdated ABC model server that has been creating problems for your company. Our team uses a different server. We use the DEF model which has more capability, is faster, and can fill all your specific needs as it has ours. Among many other capabilities available in the DEF model is GHI.

GHI capabilities are new to the server world and essential to an efficient data center. With them, you can accomplish multiple tasks such as J, K, and L. J is a feature that . . .

This technique maintains the flow and the development of ideas, and it keeps the reader interested enough to read the next paragraph.

Use Simple Language (Ninth- to Twelfth-Grade Level)

This depends on who the audience is.
Google the free online readability calculator. Cut and paste a section of your text in this online software tool. See what grade level your text is.

Don't Use Passive Language; Stay Active

Active and passive language examples below:
1. A decision has been made. (passive)
2. I made a decision. (active)
3. The new data center will be using five SupaFast servers to comply with the requirements. (passive)
4. We will use five SupaFast servers in the new data center to comply with the requirements. (active)

In sentence 4, it is also important to note that if *we* do something—especially to fix a problem—then *we* state it. It makes us active as well.

Sentences

Clear
Read it once and get it—I mean once. If the reader has to go back over the text, you messed up.

Concise
Get to the point quickly.

Correctness
Data must be technically correct.

No Hedging
"Should be able to. . . ." "It may be that. . . ." "It is possible to. . . ."
I don't use this stuff. It breeds a lack of confidence in the company and the solution.

No Grey Language or Ambiguity
Unless otherwise intentional, make a statement.

Use Modular- or Topic-Based Writing Principles
Google the term. There are lots of excellent and free PowerPoint presentations on the subject.

One Idea per Paragraph
Goes with modular. All information in the paragraph/module/topic should support or have something to do with the header directly.

Sentences Fifteen to Twenty Words in Length
Long sentences make the mind wander. Readers will tend to skip words. If a sentence is too long, the reader may have to read again to understand. And if they read again, you messed up.

Gorilla Picks on Writing Style

What Gorillas Use in Their Writing

- A style that fits the audience
- Active voice and action verbs
- Small, simple, and precise words
- Simple subject-verb-object sentences
- Simple and consistent terminology
- Descriptive text for concept topics (third person, present tense, active voice, indicative mood)
- Procedural text for task topics (second person, present tense, imperative mood, no articles)

What Gorillas Don't Use in Their Writing

- Too many acronyms in one sentence
- Quotes, italic font, bold font, underlining, or capitalization for emphasis
- Nominalizations (turning a verb, an adjective, or an adverb into a noun)
- Large words
- Words that can be contextualized differently by different readers

Definitions

Adjudicating a comment—making a determination on a comment. Incorporating it if valid, or discarding it if not.

Author—any person assigned to create a document and manage its build, review, and update. This person is solely responsible for the document and each document has only *one* author. An author can be assigned several documents. An author can be a technical writer, a PM, application architect, development lead, security architect, etc.

Authorial team—a team comprised of the author (usually an SME) and several peers that contribute material to the author's document. Sometimes called contributors or contributing authors. Though not a peer, the technical writer is usually assigned in some capacity. If the technical writer is tasked to author a document (e.g., the user guide), he/she will need to know the application thoroughly. No peer, contributor, or contributing author is considered an author of that particular document.

BRC (pronounced "brick")—"Build Review Cycle."

BRP—"Build Review Process."

Build Cycle—the process of adding data and features by document build personnel. It is the first part of the BRC process. Usually refers to the initial build of the document, but build can happen to documents that are versioned with entire sections missing. This means the blank sections would require a build. Once built, changes, mods, and additions are referred to as updates. "Build" is a finite term. You do not build a document forever (although you can update it forever). Some orgs say that, once you create a document, everything after that is an update. I distinguish between the two.

CBC—"Create, Build, Complete" (includes the BRC, complete, and sign-off).

Closed—a document is *not* accepting data, meaning it's locked prior to or after receiving data. Can be a "pens down" period, if you will. You can close a document with an email: "The following document(s) [then list them] will be closed on xx/xx/xxxx date, so get all changes in now." Or whatever. You can also close a document electronically by only allowing a "read-only" copy to be opened. Not a true workflow station.

CMS—"Content Management System."

Complete—all data has been added. Completed review cycle. Final copy/output edit is completed. Versioned. Awaiting sign-off (if necessary). Ready for delivery. "Complete" is not a finite term, as completed documents can always be updated. It just means completed for that particular delivery.

Create—to give a title, create front matter, construct the framework, make a template, and place in the proper directory (one you designate). Can also include creating workflow in spreadsheets or CMS. Not a true workflow station.

Open—a document is able and ready to accept data. Usually means it's in the workflow. Beginning of build. Example: A technical writer or author uses this term in an email: "To all team members, the XYZ document is open" (meaning they can start adding data). Or "Hey, is that document still open? I need to put stuff in it." "Yeah it's open; go ahead." Not a true workflow station.

Output/Publishing Edit—an edit conducted after a document is published to a PDF, online, or mobile format from an authoring system. I usually do these to correct format problems. From past experience, most problems were improper tagging in my authoring software. When the content is compiled and published/output in the authoring software, I can't always trust that what I see in my editor is what will come out the other end. There are parsers, style sheets (CSSs), FOs, XSLTs, schemas, and DTDs involved, and they can be picky. So if the data is improperly tagged, I don't always see it until I publish. So, I publish, conduct an output edit, and fix any problems I see (usually by retagging), then republish. There is no need for a review loop at this point, because all tech and copy edits have already been completed. Output edits can be conducted within mini reviews but *must* be done for final reviews.

Review—a technical edit, copy edit, or peer edit. To be specific, a review determines the validity of the system by reviewing a correct and true document. An edit determines the validity of the document as it relates to the system. But reviews and edits seem to be used synonymously these days, so I'll stick with "tech," "copy," and "peer."

Review cycle—the document editing loop and workflow between workflow personnel (author, SME, technical writer/editor, sign-off person, etc.). The mini review happens time and time again before delivery and is usually a continuous loop. The final review happens once before delivery, but the document keeps being cycled until all comments are adjudicated (incorporated or discarded).

Update—a change, addition, or modification to a built document; does not necessarily include a trip through the review process. However, some orgs say that, once a document has been created, everything after that is an update. As I said in the "build" definition, I distinguish between updates and build because the term "update" is too broad. It doesn't really say anything specific. I use it in the spreadsheets because it can include the following: changing existing material, deleting existing material, adding new material, or changing the sequence or structure of existing material.

Peace out.

Made in the USA
Middletown, DE
18 November 2017